Becoming a Big-picture Thinker

Without Neglecting the Details

Andrew J. DuBrin, PhD

BECOMING A BIG PICTURE THINKER

Without Neglecting the Details

Copyright@AndrewDuBrin, PhD 2019

All rights reserved.

No part of this book may be reproduced or transmitted in any form or by any means without written permission by the publisher.

Cactus Moon Publications, LLC
1305 W. 7th Street
Tempe, AZ 85281
www.cactusmoonpublishing.com

First Edition

ISBN: 978-0-9996965-9-0

Acknowledgments

My primary thanks for this project go to my executive editor at Cactus Moon Publishing, Lily Gianna Woodmansee and her staff. Lily was quick to see the possibilities in my book, and graciously offered to work with me to provide editorial suggestions and get the book into market. I thank also the many big-picture thinkers I have met in person or read about who have provided me some useful ideas for this book. Little-picture thinkers I have known contributed to this project due to the contrast with big-picture thinkers.

Writing without loved ones would be a lonely task. My thanks, therefore, also go to my family members—Drew and Heidi, Douglas and Gizella, Melanie, Drake, Rosie, Clare, Camila, Sofia, Eliana, Carson, Julian, and Owen. Thank you also to Stefanie and her daughter Sofie for their contribution to my well-being.

Preface

Becoming a Big-Picture Thinker without Neglecting the Details, deals directly with a major success factor in career and personal life. We would often accomplish much more in our job, career, and personal life if we could rise above the details of what we are doing and visualize how these details fit into the larger whole. People who can understand the purpose and broad implications of the decisions they make and the events surrounding them are frequently looked up to by others and accomplish more of significance. Despite the importance of big-picture thinking, relatively few people have developed this quality. Another problem is that many big-picture thinkers gloss over details to the extent that their big-picture scenarios cannot be executed.

This book describes relevant research and opinion about various aspects of big-picture thinking. Equally important each chapter contains suggestions for enhancing big-picture thinking, or related topics such as strategic thinking. Some of the suggestions are provided in a box insert at the end of the chapter referred to as *A Few Suggestions for Action*. Self-quizzes are presented in the first nine chapters to help the reader personalize the major idea under consideration. All key points throughout the book are illustrated with examples, including those of specific business-people and other public figures.

Chapter 1 describes in depth the meaning of big-picture thinking. The theme of the chapter is that if we could see the *big-picture* more regularly, many of us would lead a more rewarding and satisfying life. Among the explanations of big-picture thinking is that it is the main or important part of something. The chapter also describes the difference between thinking big and big-picture thinking yet thinking big also helps us see the big-picture.

Chapter 2 describes the payoffs from big-picture thinking, or why a person might want to become a big-picture thinker. Among the payoffs described are career advancement, making more intelligent decisions, creating an innovative enterprise, and being more ethical and socially responsible, and anticipating unintended consequences of your actions

Chapter 3 is about the little-picture thinker. Understanding little- picture thinking is helpful in developing your skills as a broad, long-term, strategic thinker. We present the downside of little-picture thinking including overlooking good career opportunities, staying in a rut, and being a micromanager. The silo mentality is explained as a byproduct of little-picture thinking. Narrow-mindedness is also linked to the same type of thinking.

Chapter 4 digs into the characteristics of big-picture thinker, thereby providing a focus for developing into a person who can see the big-picture. Understanding the characteristics of big-picture thinkers also enables you to work well with them. Key characteristics of big-picture thinkers include focusing more on ideas than facts, being open to experience, divergent (broad) thinking, an intuitive problem-solving style, and a passion for the work or task. Being farsighted and proactive is also typical of big-picture thinkers.

Chapter 5 describes how big-picture thinkers are able to delay gratification in order to attain a key goal, big reward, or fulfill a purpose. Delay of gratification is analyzed as being part of self-discipline, willpower, and grit. Another part of the chapter reminds us that delay of gratification is usually necessary for the big-picture of financial success.

Chapter 6 describes special skills and actions of big-picture thinkers thereby presenting more hooks for the enhancement of big-picture thinking. Among these skills and actions are minimizing minutiae, breaking the rules, frequent "eureka experiences", being a good organizational citizen, and sharing knowledge with coworkers. Big-picture thinkers are also good team players.

Chapter 7 deals with becoming a strategic thinker, a topic that continues to grow in importance because this type of thinking is considered to be an asset at all levels of the organization. Learning to think strategically involves having the right mindset, using metaphors, relevant work experience, and deep learning. Becoming a strategic thinker also involves making sure that you are working on the right problem and having good imagination. A section of the chapter explains how intuition can sometimes be sharpened by learning to look for red flags in work and personal life.

Chapter 8 explains how seeing the big-picture is a key part of effective leadership. The effective leader emphasizes macro-management in contrast to micro-management. Other components of big-picture leadership include seeing the purpose of the enterprise, being a systems thinker, self-sacrificing behavior, and seeing employees as owners. (A systems thinker sees how parts of the organization fit together, and how the organization interacts with the environment.) Treating employees well is also part of big-picture leadership.

Chapter 9 describes how big-picture thinking can help you get through setbacks and adversity. Placing the negative situation in proper perspective is at the top of the list for dealing with adversity, setback and stress. Other big-picture techniques for dealing with adversity include looking for the good within the setback, creating a vision as a path back, and meditating to help see the big-picture. The chapter also describes how big-picture thinking can be useful in getting through a crisis.

Chapter 10 is a master plan for becoming a big-picture thinker. The twenty-five suggestions presented are a compilation of key ideas presented in the previous nine chapters, along with additional ideas for enhancing big-picture thinking. Three of the new suggestions are (a) sprinkle your big-picture thinking with attention to key details that could hamper your project, (b) connect the dots by seeking to understand how your work first into or interacts with other parts of the organization, and (c) how developing your imagination will help you become a strategic, big-picture thinker.

Table of Contents

Chapter 1 1

    What is Big-Picture Thinking? 1

Chapter 2 29

    The Payoffs from Big-Picture Thinking 29

    A Few Suggestions for Action 54

Chapter 3 55

    The Little-Picture Thinker 55

Chapter 4 81

    Characteristics of Big-Picture Thinkers 81

    A Few Suggestions for Action 105

Chapter 5 107

    Big-Picture Thinking and the Delay of Gratification 107

Chapter 6 133

    Special Skills and Actions of Big-Picture Thinkers 133

    A Few Suggestions for Action 156

Chapter 7 159
   Becoming a Strategic Thinker 159
      A Few Suggestions for Action 184

Chapter 8 187
   Big-Picture Thinking and Leadership 187
      A Few Suggestions for Action 211

Chapter 9 213
   Getting Through Setbacks and Adversity 213
      A Few Suggestions for Action 237

Chapter 10 239
   A Master Plan for Becoming a Big-Picture Thinker 239

About the Author 255

Chapter 1

What is Big-Picture Thinking?

We would often accomplish much more in our job, our career, and our personal life if we could rise above the details of what we are doing and visualize how these details fit into the larger whole. Similarly, we would accomplish much more if we could conjure up an idea so big and wonderful that it would capture the imagination of many other people. If we could see the big picture more regularly, many of us would lead a more rewarding and satisfying life.

As an example of how neglecting the big picture and can block opportunities, take the case of Ashley. She is dissatisfied with her career as a research analyst in the marketing department of a major retailer. On a rainy Sunday morning, Ashley decides that this is the moment to take the first step in making a career leap. Ashley attempts to create a computer file about doing something radically different in her career. She decides to staple together a few scattered notes on index cards and the back of envelopes, she has been collecting for at least a year.

But Ashley runs into a hurdle. Her stapler is jammed, and she does not know why. So Ashley attempts to fix it. She inserts a new row of staples, the proceeds to eliminate the jam by banging the stapler several times, then prodding it with a screwdriver. She believes that you need all mechanical equipment to be operating properly before you can accomplish other work. Even with her electronic devices working well, Ashley can lose concentration if she is worried about something as mundane as a stapler.

All efforts fail for Ashley, so she drops the career planning and heads out to an office supply store to purchase a new stapler. She is frustrated and angry that her career-revitalization session did not go as planned, but she does purchase a few other needed office supplies that at the store. What happened to Ashley's aspirations? How could a non- functioning stapler throw her completely off track?

Ashley being distracted over a small matter, a defective stapler, prompted her to put away for another day imagining a career breakthrough. Perhaps this could have been the morning that Ashley conceptualized a small enterprise that would have brought her the career excitement she was seeking. Having a working stapler in her office at home is certainly a small detail that needs attention, but it should have been given low priority this morning.

To illustrate an extraordinary example of big-picture thinking, we choose Elon Musk[1], who has been referred to as the modern-day Thomas Edison. Musk was one of the founders of PayPal then went on to become the founder and CEO of Tesla, and SpaceX, and the chairman of SolarCity. In 2015, at age 44, he held a public gathering at the Tesla design studio in

Hawthorne, California. Musk walked onto the stage as hard rock music blared in the background. He began his presentation by showing an image of thick, yellowish smoke pouring out of a number of industrial chimneys. At the same time, Musk displayed a chart indicating how an accumulation of carbon dioxide in the air is moving the earth toward an almost inevitable calamity. He informed the crowd, "What I am going to talk about tonight is a fundamental transformation of how the world works."

The purpose of the meeting was to launch a new product line of large batteries that store energy in homes, plus even larger batteries that that store energy for utilities and businesses. For a medium-picture thinker, the meeting would have focused on this new line of batteries. Yet for the big-picture-thinking Elon Musk, the evening presentation was about changing the world. An additional grand purpose of the new line of batteries was to eliminate the world's dependence on power plants.

A closer look at the meaning of big-picture thinking.

1. The term *big-picture thinking* has several closely-related definitions and meanings. A good starting point is to recognize that a big-picture thinker is a conceptual thinking—he or she has an overall or global perspective on a situation. The little-picture retail executive thinks, "If we can close two more stores in the Chicago area, we can save four million per year in annual operating costs." The big-picture executive says, "True, we can save four-million in operating costs per year, yet there is a cost. Each store that stays open functions like a permanent

advertisement. It reinforces in the consumer's mind that our chain exists, and that we are conveniently located."

The big picture has also been defined as the main or important part of something. A person is said to be a big-picture thinker when he or she can understand a situation or concept as a whole rather than getting bogged down in specific details. Similarly the big-picture thinker gets the gist of something without getting caught in the details.[2]

2. A couple might be contemplating the purchase of a 300-year-old armoire at an antique store. The detail-oriented husband says, "Forget this ragged old armoire. I see three scratches and one chip." The big-picture-thinking wife says, "This is a magnificent piece of furniture that will blend in perfectly with our other antiques. A few small imperfections do not detract from its beauty and value."

Big-picture thinking can also be described as the way a person perceives problems, opportunities, and situations. A big-picture thinker will often generate many alternative solutions to problems. He or she is likely to be an idea-generator who thinks of huge changes, large projects, and opportunities to start a new business. Big-picture thinking often leads to creativity, and innovation.[3]

3. The effective big-picture thinker might rely on others to execute his or her big ideas but does not totally neglect the details. Elon Musk, for example, may be an extraordinary big

thinker, yet he also makes decision about design details such as the configuration of the dashboard on the Tesla.

An analogy can be drawn between big-picture thinking and the direction of a play. A blogger wrote that if she is the director of a play, she would not be able to see the whole representation or gestalt of a scene if she were on stage directing mixed in with the characters. "Seated off stage in the audience or even in the balcony, I can see the bigger picture of how the actors engage with each other, the lighting, the set design, and the sound quality. I can see things I wouldn't be able to if I didn't set myself apart to view the big picture."[4]

Ben Carson, the former director of pediatric neurosurgery at Johns Hopkins Children Center, and more recently the Secretary of Housing and Urban Development (HUD), has another concept of the big picture.

According to Carson, the big picture is a vision of something truly worth living for, something that calls forth the best of a person's talents, energy, and focus.[5]

4. A big picture, according to this meaning is an important and worthy purpose, such as having a career that helps other people of building a hospital in a poor neighborhood whose population is underserved medically.

To pursue a big picture of this lofty nature, a person does not have to occupy a position of power or earn a high income. For example, a kindergarten teacher might have what she perceives to be one of the most important purposes in her life. She might explain, "One of my responsibilities to get five-year-old children on the path to becoming good readers. Without my help these children could never escape poverty or live a comfortable life."

Although Carson's meaning of the big picture may be lofty, it still refers to a big picture of taking an overall perspective on what we are doing. At the same time, the big picture considers the purpose of an activity.

The accompanying self-quiz provides you an opportunity to reflect on your present tendencies toward big-picture thinking.

My Tendencies toward Big-Picture Thinking

Indicate your strength of agreement with each of the following statements: SD - strongly disagree; D – disagree; N – neutral, A – agree; SA –strongly agree.

	SD	D	N	A	SA
1. I get upset if my checkbook does not balance even to the dollar.	5	4	3	2	1
2. I often think about the meaning and implication of news stories.	1	2	3	4	5
3. A top-level manager is usually better off finding ways to cut costs than thinking about the future of the business.	5	4	3	2	1
4. I like to argue (or used to) with an instructor about what should be the correct answer to a multiple- choice question.	5	4	3	2	1
5. So long as a company provides good customer service with its	5	4	3	2	1

present product line, its future is very secure.					
6. I prefer acquiring knowledge and skills that can help me with my job during the next month rather than those that might help me in the future.	5	4	3	2	1
7. It makes me laugh when a CEO says a big part of his or her job is creating visions.	5	4	3	2	1
8. I have already created a vision for my life.	1	2	3	4	5
9. I am a "big-picture" thinker.	1	2	3	4	5
10. If people take care of today's problems, they do not have to worry about the future.	5	4	3	2	1
11. World events have very little impact on my life.	5	4	3	2	1
12 An organization cannot become great with an exciting vision.	1	2	3	4	5

Scoring and interpretation: Find your total score by summing the point values for each question.

52 – 60: You probably already a big-picture thinker which should help you in our career.

30 – 51: You probably have a neutral, detached attitude toward thinking big.

12 – 29: Your thinking probably emphasizes the here and now and the short term. People in this category usually do not focus on the implications of their work.

Big-Picture Thinking and Treating Retail Workers Well

The treatment of retail workers by their employers presents an interesting application of big-picture thinking. Many retail executives, as well as store owners, contend that they cannot afford to give many retail clerks full-time jobs or pay them relatively high wages for several reasons. A major reason is that high wages lead to high prices, and consumers tend to shop by price. Another reason is that profit margins are so thin in many retail operations, that paying high wages and benefits would be unprofitable. For many retailers, including restaurant operations, this reasoning is true. If a locally-owned convenience store paid its checkout clerks, $30 per hour in wages and benefits, the store could not afford to remain in business.

The research of Zeynep Ton, an associate adjunct professor of operations management at the MIT Sloan School of Management, disagrees with the logic just presented.[6] The research she conducted for over ten years takes a big-picture perspective on the importance of treating retail workers generously. Ton has found that the strongly-believed trade-off between investment in employees and low prices can be overcome. Several highly successful retail chains, including Quik-Trip convenience stores, Trader Joe's, and Costco Wholesale Club pay their employees relatively well, and offer very low prices. At the same time these stores are quite profitable and offer better customer service than their competitors.

These successful retail chains have demonstrated that even in a low-price segment of retail, low-paying, part-time jobs are a cost- driven necessity, but a choice. And they have demonstrated that the key to overcoming the trade-off is a combination of investment in the workforce, and business practices that benefit employees, customers, as well as the company. Part of Ton's big-picture thinking is that the United States needs better jobs, not just more job.

Ton has found that successful retailers engage in four operational practices that complement their investment in employees. In combination, these practices make the execution of work more efficient and more fulfilling for employees, lower costs, improve customer service, and boost sales and profits. A major contribution of these practices is to enable retailers to break the strongly-believed tradeoff between investing in employees and offering low prices.

1. *Offer less variety of merchandise.* A high product variety often adds costs up and down the supply chain, including the store being stuck with unsold inventory. The operating environment becomes more complex for store employees without necessarily increasing sales. With fewer products, store associates can be familiar with more items sold in the store and make informed recommendations to customers.

2. *Achieve flexibility by cross-training employees.* The purpose of cross-training workers is so that they can perform many tasks instead of varying the number of employees to match

changes in the amount of customer traffic. Part-time retail workers frequently get quite short notices of changes in their work schedule and are sometimes told to go home before their shifts end. Even worse from the standpoint of employee mistreatment, some workers are supposed to reserve time just to be available for notice to report to work. Being "on hold" for a low-paying job qualifies as mistreatment by many workers.

3. *Eliminate waste in everything but staffing.* Another approach to keeping in mind the big picture of treating employees well is to be highly efficient in as many aspects of store operations as possible. By being more efficient from an operations standpoint, workers are less rushed and have more time to serve customers well. An example of eliminating waste would be the Costco practice of selling merchandise directly from pallets, thereby requiring much less handling loading and unloading of merchandise. Eliminating waste by minimizing the staffing of stores saves some money but results in poorer customer service and many employees being overworked.

4. *Empower employees to make small on-the-spot decisions.* Customer service and employee satisfaction is increased when employees are empowered to make small decisions about product returns and customer complaints. If a plastic bag broke in the parking lot, for example, the cashier might have the authority to replace items that were damaged or destroyed by falling to the ground.

The big-picture thinking about treating employees well in order to do a social good and enhance profits has merits and increases the odds but does not guarantee success. Competitive forces, such as an increase in online shopping or the emergence of discount chains can suck the profits away from a large retail chain. An even when the big-picture thinking executive wants to elevate the status of store associates, some little thinking will be necessary to monitor the humane approach. For example, a small problem with empowering retail workers to grant returns without question is that some store associates will be overly-generous in granting returns to friends and family members.

Thinking Big and Big-Picture Thinking

Thinking big has long been woven into the self-help movement. People are advised that if they think big, good things will happen to them. Thinking big has even been described as the one major factor that separates successful people from their less successful counterparts.[7] The idea of thinking big also suggests that if you set your goals high and you will achieve them, and that you can achieve almost anything you want if establish the right goals. Thinking big has its merits in helping us set high goals, but thinking big must also be accompanied by talent, experience, and self-discipline for thinking big to result in accomplishment rather than wishful thinking. (Self-discipline in this context refers to concentrated effort to accomplish a goal, such as sticking with learning a second language until a reasonable level of proficiency has been attained.)

Setting High Goals. Thinking big in order to succeed has been a popular subject of books, articles, and websites for many years. *The Magic of Thinking Big,* by David Schwartz stands out as a pioneering book in the thinking-big movement. The book emphasizes the now well-recognized approach to success of setting high goals, and then thinking positively to facilitate attaining these goals. (Yes, the power of positive thinking in yet another version.)

A bedrock principle of thinking big is to think positively toward oneself, often by raising one's expectations. An intermediate-level tennis player who enters a city tournament, might think to herself, "If I play at my best, I think I can get to the third round." The high self-expectations for the tennis player give her a spurt of self-confidence that might help her play at the top of her game and facilitate two wins in the tournament.

Visualizing success. Visualization is another part of thinking big in the form of thinking what can be, not just what already exists. The owner of a startup restaurant might visualize his restaurant being filled with customers even though there are several other restaurants on the same block. Just fantasizing about this possibility will most likely have no impact on the restaurant being a success. Yet the visualization might prompt the restaurant owner to take steps to make the visualization become a reality. These steps would include creating an attractive window display or sending e-mail and text messages to everybody he and his staff know, inviting the e-mail and text message recipients to give the restaurant a try.

Transmitting good news. Schwartz also encourages people to broadcast good news as part of thinking big. Transmitting good news to other people makes the transmitter feel better, and the good news also has a positive effect on other people. The payoff from this aspect of thinking big is more satisfaction with life, and the establishment of better relationships with people because the feel better in one's presence. An exception, however, is that some people are happier to hear about your misfortune and tend to envy good fortune. But the big thinker recognizes that you cannot please everybody.[8]

Empowering Language. The language you use regularly is a testimony of your thinking with respect to thinking big or small. If your expressed thoughts are riddled with complaining, worrying, and sharp criticisms of your life circumstances, your life will reflect these words. If you take the opposite approach by using empowering words and phrases that focus on solutions, and expanding possibilities, your life will probably reflect these thoughts.[9] For example, a person whose debt is too high might say, "I see need for improvement here. Starting now, I will find a way to reduce expenses by $200 per month and invest that amount in debt reduction."

Empowering language, or the opposite, can be regarded as self-fulfilling prophesies. If you continue to think small about yourself you will minimize taking on activities at work or personal life that will move your forward, In contrast, if you make positive self-statements, you will become more confident and willing to engage in activities that will move your forward.

Breaking through limitations we set for ourselves. Michael Port, a motivational specialist, believes that in order to thrive, we have to let go of self-imposed limitations, and give things a try.[10] Among these self-imposed limitations that block us from thinking big are as follows:
- A company that well-known would never hire me.
- My idea for a new business is far too risky.
- Without an MBA I will never get promoted.
- A popular person like that would never go out with me.

Part of breaking through limitations is to set goals that stretch your capability but are nevertheless possibly attainable because they are realistic. An entry-level professional at an investment bank might think big by aspiring to become a partner in the firm within seven years. An unrealistic approach to thinking big would be establish-ing a two-year target for becoming a partner. A self-imposed limitation for the entry- level professional would be to think, "I'm not talented enough to ever become partner in this firm."

Surround yourself with big thinkers and doers. Dreams can sometimes be converted to reality by spending time with people who are already doing what you aspire to accomplish, or your big thoughts. This technique of surrounding yourself with awesome people is substantiated by social learning theory which suggests that much of our learning and motivation stems from observing other people. It may be difficult to find people in your immediate network who share your big thoughts, so you might seek out people in the social media, read books and articles about people who lead the life you aspire toward, or join online forums in your field.[11]

How thinking big helps us see the big picture. Thinking big centers on setting big goals and harboring positive attitudes—both are standard bromides for personal success and happiness. Thinking big also has a payoff because it helps us see the big picture. If you think big, you have established a grand goal, and quite often that grand goal is part of the big picture. Imagine the situation of Roberto, the director of facilities planning at a medium-size company. He is responsible for the company relocating headquarters to another region where taxes and energy costs are lower, and wages are lower because of a lower cost of living.

Roberto and his staff have to suffer through hundreds of details that are essential to accomplishing the move. Among these are such matters as changing the company address on all company communications, hiring new staff to replace those employees who choose not to relocate, purchasing office furniture, and installing the information technology infrastructure in the new location. The frustration associated with this myriad of tasks is easier to endure when Roberto and his staff think of the big picture of a sparkling new company location with all its associated benefits.

Visualizing How Your Job Fits into the Big-picture
One of the most practical applications of big-picture thinking is to visualize, or understand, how your job fits into the purpose of your organization. Understanding how your job contributes to the organization helps elevate job satisfaction and performance. It is easier to be happy and perform better when you understand how you are contributing to the good of the organization and to other people. Kaitlin is a mechanical engineer working for a manufacturer of escalators and elevators, so it does not take much visualization for her understand how her role contributes to the big picture. Kaitlin expresses the reality, "How could you construct an elevator or escalator without the input of a mechanical engineer? I wouldn't want a friend or family member to ride in or on such a device."

Visualizing how your role contributes to the organizational purpose also offers a political advantage. If you mention to influential people that you are contributing to the total organizational effort, you are likely to perceived as a strategic thinker (a high-level compliment). Strategic thinking is such an important part of seeing the big picture that it receives separate attention in Chapter 7, and the term will be mentioned frequently throughout the book.

Task significance is the technical term given to one aspect of how a position fits into the big picture. The term refers to the degree to which a job affects the lives of other people. The more tasks significance built into a job, the easier it is to see the big picture. Take the case of Byron, a production technician who assembles smoke detectors for home and industrial use. He can readily understand how his work impacts the lives of other people. If Byron does a faulty job that gets past the quality inspectors, the lives of people, as well as those of some domestic animals, could be perish in a fire. If he helps construct flawless smoke detectors, many lives will be saved in homes, restaurants, offices, and hotels.

Seeing how one's job fits into the big picture can also be framed as developing the right perspective or understanding how your proposal might affect other parts of the organization.[12] Jennifer, a human resource specialist, might observe that uncovering unconscious biases in selecting job candidates, and giving assignments and promotions to current employees, is a hot topic in human resource management. Jennifer therefore proposes every manager and supervisor in the company attend during working hours a couple of seminars about unconscious biases in the work-place. Her proposal is admirable, but she is not carefully examining the big picture. Jennifer has not considered how much time would be taken from other productive work if the seminars she proposes were implemented.

Leadership specialist, James G. Clawson, explains that the movement toward subcontracting and virtual organizations is making it more difficult for many employees to see how their work fits into the total organization or big picture.[13] Instead of seeing a manager or supervisor face-to face many workers now rely on electronic communication to interact with bosses, and often coworkers. A subcontractor in New Delhi, India might be performing some legal research for a large legal firm in New

York. It might be difficult for the subcontractor to understand how his or her small chunk of work helps the large legal firm run smoothly.

Big-Picture Thinking as Strategic Thinking

The term *strategy* has several different definitions with the popular one referring to a person's technique or approach for getting something accomplished. For example: A person might say, "My strategy for keeping ants out of my kitchen is to sweep the floor twice a day to get rid of crumbs, and spray ant-killer poison on the floor." Strategy in reference to business and related activities also has several meanings. As used here, strategy refers to an integrated overall concept of how the organization will attain its objectives. Strategy is therefore a master plan for getting big things done. An example of a business strategy is "sticking to core competency." The organization focuses its effort on what it does best to become world class. A sterling example is the watch company Citizen that manufactures and sells only watches and has been in business since 1930.

An amusing, but telling, illustration of how big-picture thinking is tied in with strategic thinking is the story behind the Aflac Duck®. Daniel P. Amos, now the chairman of Aflac (originally, American Family Assurance Company) writes that the origins of the ubiquitous duck go back to the year 2000. At the time, the American Family Life Assurance company was suffering from low name recognition. A radical name change would have required obtaining new insurance licenses in every state, so the company decided on Aflac. The creative group at a New York advertising agency came up with the idea of the Aflac Duck because they had difficulty remembering the company name. One day an advertising copy writer asked, "What is the name of the account we're pitching?" A colleague replied, "It's Aflac, Aflac, Aflac." Someone said he sounded like a duck, and the idea for the advertising campaign was born.

The Aflac Duck scored well in tryouts by the advertising agency, and the light went on for Amos. He sensed that this duck could somehow help Aflac attain its strategic goals of becoming a leading insurance company. When Amos mentioned the Aflac Duck to other executives, all he received was a silent stare. Amos then decided to tell colleagues only that he had decided on a new advertising campaign that attained amazing numbers in preliminary testing.

Visualizing the potential of the duck-themed advertising campaign, Amos decided to run the commercial for two weeks and carefully monitor the results. The first Aflac Duck ad was launched on New Year's Day, 2000, on CNN, and ran four times per hour. Again seeing the big picture, Amos sensed that businesspeople would be watching CNN regularly to see if the Y2K virus was really going to severely damage computer systems. Overwhelming success was attained immediately. On the first day of the telecast, the company had more visits to its website than in the entire year before. Within weeks, Aflac was getting requests for a stuffed animal version of the duck. A subcontractor was hired to manufacture the ducks, and all the proceeds were donated to the Aflac Cancer Center in Atlanta.

The Aflac Duck was also a sensation when displayed at an event at Disney studios (even though Donald Duck is king at Disney). Amos knew he had a winner, but the big question remained of whether the Aflac Duck would help the company attain its business goals. The answer was affirmative, with first year sales in the United States up by 29 percent and increased by 100 percent in three years. Today the name recognition of Aflac is higher than 90 percent.

Aflac was then brought to the Japanese market in 2009 when the company's Japanese marketing team introduced a new version of the duck for a new insurance product. The duck was a blend of the North American duck and the traditional Asian good luck white cat, Maneki Neko. The commercial focused on the cat duck was an enormous success in terms of rated popularity, and increased Aflac revenues by 44 percent over a seven-year period. More than one-half of the company's revenues stem from Japan.

The Aflac Duck story is certainly impressive, but for the present purpose, the big-picture thinking of Daniel P. Amos must be scrutinized. Before moving forward with the campaign, Amos reasoned: "Having gotten my college degrees in risk management, I was committed to making the decision the way I'd been taught: Don't risk a lot for a little; don't risk more than you can afford to lose; and consider the odds." The plan was to invest one million in the initial campaign, an affordable sum for the company. Amos also felt that the odds were reasonable of getting a good return on the money invested. The big picture was moving Aflac forward on a grand scale, and the little picture was squandering one million and some executive time.[14]

Strategy applies to the individual. The business concept of strategy also has considerable relevance to the individual. The majority of successful people did not attain their goals through simply working hard and being lucky. Instead, they had an overall plan for success including establishing career goals, obtaining the right formal education, continuous learning, and building a network of valuable contacts. Many of these people got the big picture early in life, such as studying a second language seriously in high school to better fit in the new global economy.

An individual within a firm who is not part of top-level management can also profit from thinking strategically and looking at the big picture. Leanne Hoagland-Smith observes that the highest performing sales professionals schedule time to plan, strategize, and think. They think of the long-term, such as "Am I getting the most out of my territory?"

They also ponder whether they are investing their time in the areas that produce the greatest return. Successful sales representatives look at each sales opportunity strategically, starting with their goal in mind. They develop tactics to get them to the end goal as quickly and effectively as possible. Should surprises happen, rather than reacting impulsively, they pause to under-stand, and adjust their strategies as needed.

Top sales professional understands the value of planning in such areas as planning a sales call, planning to make a deal, planning how to maximize growth in their territory, and planning how to most effectively spend their time. Strategic thinking is the way top sales approach every aspect of their job. Understanding the big picture is what separates the high-level sales professionals from their counterparts chasing transactions.[15]

Most organizations would benefit if a wide range of employees looked at the big picture—and therefore strategic— impact of their activities. Have you even been automatically given a plastic bag when making a small purchase such as a tube of lipstick, four AAA batteries, or a candy bar? If the checkout clerk recognized that every plastic bag not used would cut expenses by one or two cents, and also help maintain a less clogged environment, the company and the country would be better off. A representative of a training and strategy consulting firm asks this question:

Imagine if every employee and leader considered the environmental context in which they operate, the resources they have at their disposal, the relationships they need to foster, and the most efficient way to operate as to achieve the best results and sustain them. Can any organization today afford not to enable or encourage such a process?[16]

Asking big-picture questions as part of strategic thinking. The big-picture thinker who contributes to business strategy not only has some grand ideas of his or her own, but also asks questions that enhance the big-picture thinking of others. If you have formal authority, such as being a high-level manager, others are more likely to answer your questions. Yet, asking such questions of coworkers, and even your boss, will also enhance your skills and reputation as a strategic thinker. Here are a few provocative big-picture questions:[17]

- Why is your idea important?
- What will be the impact of your project on the rest of the organization?
- If your project is not approved, how will this hurt the organization?
- Who cares about your proposal? Who will be affected both directly and indirectly?

After these big-picture questions are answered, the effective strategic thinker responds to the answers in a thoughtful way. For example: "I agree that outsourcing our manufacturing of American flags to Mexico would save us considerable money in labor costs, but let's also talk about the potential negative publicity for our company."

Mega-Goals and the Big-Picture

An elegant way of looking at the big picture is to establish mega-goals. Such goals are so big and have such heavy positive outcomes if reached that transcend lesser goals in work and personal life. A mega-goal can also be regarded a superordinate goal—an overarching goal that captures the imagination of people. The superordinate goal is similar to a vision because it relates to an idea and is often inspirational. The construction manager of a water-treatment company might explain that "We are working together to improve water quality and help rid the world of deadly diseases stemming from contaminated water."

Another one of Elton Musk's initiatives provides a germane example of a mega-goal. The train system that SpaceX is building is labeled the Hyperloop. Transporting people in a giant tube at speeds of approximately 700 miles per hour will mean traveling from London to Edinburg or Los Angeles to San Francisco is less than 30 minutes, (This big-picture time estimate does not include getting to the Hyperloop station and the time spent checking in and boarding.)

The Hyperloop is a futuristic train that Musk describes as "a cross between a Concorde, a railgun, and an air hockey table." The Hyperloop is based on a very high-speed transit system originally proposed in 1972, and combines a magnetic levitation train a low pressure transit tube. The Hyperloop resembles that vacuum system that was formerly widely-used in banks and department stores to transport money and documents internally.[18]

We consider the building of the Hyperloop to be a mega-goal and big-picture thinking because it would be uplifting for employees to visualize the end product actually being used by travelers. The development of the Hyperloop also provides an example of how looking at the little picture or details, will make the big picture or mega-goal possible. Somebody has to work out the details of making sure cars, trucks, and people do not cross the rails over which the Hyperloop flies as it passes through town. Another key detail would be to ensure that the Hyperloop does not depart from its designated travel path. The impact of a giant steel tube hitting anything at 700 miles per hour would be a disaster. An additional small-picture detail to be managed, would be dealing with the problem of a passenger who wanted to visit the restroom in a tube moving faster than a jetliner. And finally, the cost of the Hyperloop might prove to be prohibitive. A 350-mile path between Los Angeles and San Francisco is fore-casted to cost at least six billion.

Disruptions as Big-Picture Thinking

An aspect of big-picture thinking that has permeated society is disruptive innovation. The term refers to the way a new product or service transforms an existing market by bringing new simplicity, convenience, and affordability. Famous disruptions include PCs decreasing the demand mainframe computers, tablet computers decreasing the demand for PCs, and mobile phones decreasing the demand for landline telephones and small computers. Another publicized disruption is taxi-hailing services, such as Uber and Lyft that decrease the demand for taxis and salaried taxi-cab drivers. A less publicized disruption is sports clothing manufacturers selling directly to consumers, decreasing the demand for retail stores selling their clothing lines.

Technology-based disruptions reflect big-picture thinking because the disrupter looks at an existing product or industry, and reflects on such issues as:

- "How could this service be changed in a revolutionary way?"

- "Isn't it time for people to get the same service more quickly and at a lower price?"
- "Why do we need such large-size machines to per-form a small task?"
- Why not put a gadget in people's hands that could accomplish thousands of tasks?

Disrupters are not necessarily the first to market with a new invention or service. Yet they are big-picture thinkers and visionaries who understand how an existing idea can be made less expensively or accessible to millions of people.[19] An example of a disrupter on a less grandiose scale is Keir Dillon who was the first to develop colorful, stylish headphones to replace the basic, monochrome type. Ten years later, he and his team at their company called Frends, offer premium headphones for women that are treated much like designer handbags. The headphones are wrapped in soft leather and are accented with hand-polished antiqued metals.

Dillon says, "We have a humanized approach to design. We want to use materials people can relate to, like leather, denim, cashmere, and then integrate vintage metalworking and jewelry-making techniques." Furthermore, the headphones have been positioned as a desirable accessory instead of a strictly functional tech device. (The big-picture thinking here is seeing a grand purpose for headphones in addition to just being a listening device.)

A Few Suggestions for Action

Implementing the following suggestions is likely to enhance your ability to see the big picture.

1. Stay informed about the outside world. Being closely aware of current events helps a person develop a broader viewpoint that could apply to work and personal life.

2. Read outside your specialty field. Many big-picture thinkers poke into new fields to broaden their thinking.

3. A big picture is more likely to emerge when you dig for many alternatives to a problem facing you.

4. Thinking big (or having lofty goals) will often trigger your thinking about the relevant big picture of what you are attempting. Your big goal will often be part of the big picture.

5. You are likely to be more satisfied with your job and build as stronger reputation by understanding how your job or role fits into the big picture of your employer.

6. Force yourself to be cognizant of details that could hamper your big-picture project, such as the entrepreneur who is so occupied with pursuing a dream that he neglects to pay bills on time. He thereby damages his creditworthiness and is denied access to a loan he needs to continue his project.

Chapter 2

The Payoffs from Big-Picture Thinking

Why bother searching for the big picture when it requires much less mental and emotional energy to be concerned just about details and the present? Don't you already have enough to do in life? Big-picture thinking is important because it has valuable payoffs in work and personal life. The big-picture thinker can often rise above the grueling details of the moment and see the long- term positive outcome of the details. Big-picture thinking can also help people advance their careers, have more fun on the job, make more intelligent decisions, and behave more ethically. All of these benefits are the subject of this chapter, and here are a couple of examples to illustrate the payoffs from big-picture thinking.

A CEO dealing with a costly and time-consuming product recall might be able to employ big-picture thinking and say, "This recall is ugly, and will cost us millions. But soon the thousands of customers who love our brand will either forgive us or forget the recall. Our company is damaged, but not undone."

A homeowner who is moving from one home to another that is more spacious and luxurious will inevitably be embroiled in dozens of difficult tasks. These include changes of addresses, notifying the utility company, packing, and getting the present home updated enough to pass inspection by the mortgage provider. While the homeowner is working with the significant other in clearing the attic and garage, it would be tempting to think, "Why did we ever get involved in this self-imposed misery? I am stressed, and my body aches from all this lifting, throwing out junk, and packing." Yet with a little effort directed toward big-picture thinking, a pleasant scenario surfaces: "In a month from now we will laugh at all the inconvenience. We will be in a home that is more comfortable and spacious. Our children will love the school they can walk to, as well as playing in a bigger backyard."

Career Advancement

A major payoff from big-picture thinking is that it facilitates career advancement in several ways. People who can visualize a sensible big picture are more likely to advance in their careers than their counterparts who focus on the small picture. An example of a small-picture thinker who does not experience much career advancement is the critic who frequently finds fault with the creative ideas of others. Instead of proposing useful ideas of his or her own, he or she just snipes at others, establishing a negative image that blocks his or her being promoted.

Suitability for promotion. As people are evaluated for purposes of promotion into positions of more managerial responsibility, a frequent qualification for promotion is the ability to see the big picture.[20] As the level of the position increases in responsibility, the demand for the prospect's ability to take a conceptual, overall perspective also increases.

Senior management positions tend to require a considerable amount of big-picture thinking. For example a restaurant executive might have to ponder about the impact of a big increase in minimum hourly pay will have on the profitability of stores owned by franchisees.

The call to action here, for someone looking to move up in an organizational hierarchy, would be to display big-picture thinking when appropriate. Mia, a product manager in the pet food division of a grocery company might state in a meeting, "I'm thinking of introducing a vitamin-laced cat food, but would that product lower the demand for our standard cat-food offerings?" Or Mia might ask, "What would veterinarians think of cat food heavy in vitamins?"

A related way of demonstrating big-picture thinking is to understand and articulate how your job fits into the overall organization. This approach is also referred to as systems thinking because it recognizes that each task performed in an organization is linked to its purpose. Dylan, a mechanical engineer for a company that manufactures flashlights and batteries, proposes an advanced design for the flashlight switch. He explains in a report that although the new design might add twenty-five cents to the cost of producing a flashlight, it will have a substantial impact on the sales of the battery division.

Dylan writes, "A big reason many people don't use or throw away a flashlight is that it will no longer turn on. They might buy new batteries once for a flashlight that does not work, but they then stop using the flashlight. Nobody will bother buying batteries for a flashlight that no longer works."

The career vision statement. A specific technique for facilitating career advancement through big-picture thinking is to create a career vision. As developed by career specialist Randall S. Hansen, a career vision is a statement that describes what you want to achieve in your career.[21] The statement includes the major accomplishments you hope to attain, the position you hope to attain, and the impact on others you would like to make.

A key reason that a career vision statement is big-picture thinking is that it projects you to a lofty place in your career, even if the distance from the present to that ideal future is considerable. By explicitly stating your vision, you initiate a process that increases the chances of you eventually achieving your goal. A career vision statement alerts you to what is possible and gives you a tangible end to work toward.

A career vision statement looks is also big-picture related because it creates a mental image of the future, rather than describing who you are now. The vision statement focuses on the peak of your career that will take place sometime in the future. For many people the peak of their career is not necessarily the final position in their career. For example, a junior high school teacher might envision becoming a school superintendent in his mid-forties, but then return to the classroom by her mid-fifties. Or how about becoming a CEO at age 50, and after that operating a food truck from age sixty forward?

Hansen advises that the career vision statement is the highest goal you want for your career. The goal should be one that inspires, energizes, motivates, and keeps pushing you toward its attainment. Individual preferences and capabilities will determine the exact nature of the goal. The peak goal for one person might chief financial officer of a Fortune 500 company, for another person of similar education and talent the goal might be to own and operate a bookstore.

Deciding on your career goal may take time, but the process can be simple, according to career coach Deborah Brown-Volkman. She says, "All of life's journeys begin with the phrase, 'I want.' It's a very powerful phrase, and without it, it's hard to go very far."[22]

While preparing a career vision statement, you are advised to be optimistic and not too practical minded. As you move toward attaining your big-picture thinking about your career, you can adjust to necessary details, such as obtaining the necessary financing for starting a business. Choose from among the following questions that appear most relevant to your circumstances, and answer them with the best information you have now: [23]

1. What would be career nirvana for me?
2. What is my definition of career success?
3. What kind of work would I do right now if I had all the money I needed for the rest of my life?
4. What type of work or position would I choose if I had the power to make the choice?
5. What type of company would I want to work for?

6. If I worked for a company, what type of organizational culture would I want the company to have?

7. At my retirement party, what would I like people to say I accomplished during my career?

8. Which several people do I think have an ideal position right now?

a. What is it about their careers that I consider to be ideal?

b. Which aspect of their work might I incorporate into my career vision?

9. Not worrying about money or being practical, what type of work would be ideal for me?

10. What is my strongest talent, and how could I include that talent into my career vision?

11. What is my favorite activity related to work or personal life, and how might I include that activity in my career vision?

12. In which aspect of my work do I out-perform most people?

13 How would this talent fit into my career vision?

Consolidate your answers to the questions you chose and prepare (a) a statement of your career vision in about twenty-five words, and (b) a two-page story about you at the peak of your career.

Another recommendation Hansen offers is to avoid vision killers as you go through the career-visioning process. Among these deterrents are fear of ridicule, short-term thinking, too narrow a focus, or pursuing a traditional career goal that you find to be uninspiring.

Two examples of brief career-vision statements follow. Similar to company vision statements, a statement of approximately twenty- five to fifty words is likely to be most effective. Keeping the vision statement handy, such as in a stored e-mail or text message to yourself will help you stay focused on your career goal:

- To become the founder and CEO of a homebuilding company that builds affordable, high quality homes to replace abandoned homes in deteriorating sections of cities. Our company will create many job opportunities for previously unemployed people in the communities we serve. The homes we build will help improve the neighborhoods in which they are located.

- I want to earn approximately one million per year trading stocks, bonds, and currencies working alone in a Brooklyn condominium overlooking Wall Street. My lavish lifestyle will be the envy of my real friends as well as virtual friends on the social media.

Notice that we are not taking sides by implying that career vision statements have to be strong on social responsibility. But we do emphasize that these vision statements look at the big picture.

More Meaningful and Satisfying Work

To the extent that a person sees how his or her work fits into the big picture, that person's work will be more meaningful and satisfying, as was implied in Chapter 1. If your role within an organization, or as a self-employed individual, fits your life's purpose, your job satisfaction will most likely increase. The complexity in the statement just made is that you must first have an overall purpose, or big picture for the source of job satisfaction to be present.

For many workers, their overall purpose is to make the world a better place, with improving the world taking many different forms depending on the person's values and perspective. One person whose work involves a crusade against using animal furs for clothing might think that she is making the world a better place, Yet, from the perspective of many Eskimos and Inuit, she is making the world a crueler place. These inhabitants of the North Pole region make their living by hunting seals and bears. Being deprived of the small amounts of money they make as hunters, creates misery for them.

Later in this chapter we describe how corporate social responsibility fits into the big picture. Yet your work does not have to involve corporate social responsibility, such as a company helping to rebuild poor neighborhoods, to be engaged in meaningful work. If you think big, you will probably be able to figure out why your job makes an impact on people, and therefore has meaning. Here are a few examples of understanding the meaning of work in positions that are not usually linked to social responsibility:

- Margot is an investor at a hedge fund. She is aware of the negative publicity hedge funds have received in recent years. Margot has a different take on the impact of her work: "Because of the winning investments we make, we are able to lend money to many enterprises that creates jobs and improve people's lives.

Just last month, we financed the construction of two different assisted-living apartment buildings. I think that helping people be comfortable and semi-independent in their final years is a great purpose of my work."

- Clayton is a roofing technician, who climbs up on the top of houses to help repair or replace roofs, often when the temperature is very cold or very hot. Asked why his work is important, Clayton says, "Are you kidding? If a roof goes so does the whole house. Water leaks are a killer. They look terrible and they destroy the plaster and the support beams."
- Abigail is a middle manager at an international candy maker. She describes the impact and importance of her work in these terms: "A lot of people think that candy isn't so important. They even blame us in part for the obesity epidemic. But I have a different take on what we do at our company. I help implement the plans of top management. If our plans aren't implemented, the candy is not sold and distributed. Candy brings a lot of happiness to millions of people, at a very low price. For a dollar candy-bar, a person can feel euphoric for a few minutes. That's hard to beat."

In short, a person who reflects carefully on the big-picture implications of his or her work will often find the work to be meaningful. As a result, the person will experience more job satisfaction.

Making More Intelligent Decisions

A major payoff from seeing the big picture is that it frequently leads to more intelligent decisions. If you consider such factors as why the decision you are making is significant, and the long-range consequences of your decision, the decision you make is likely to be more beneficial. Intuition is a major contributor to understanding the big picture of a contemplated decision.

The term intuition requires clarification to differentiate it from wild, undisciplined hunches, or gut feels. Intuition is an experienced-based way of knowing or reasoning in which weighing and balancing evidence are done unconsciously and automatically. Intuition is also a way of arriving at a conclusion without using the step-by-step logical process.[24] Intuition can be mostly on experience or mostly on feeling.[25]

The fact that experience contributes to intuition means that you can become more intuitive by solving many different problems because accumulated facts are an asset to intuition. It also means that you will have better intuition if you perform the same work for a relatively long period of time.[26] Having made similar decisions in the past will help you use intuition in the service of looking at the big picture when faced with a major decision.

The suggestion surfaces frequently that to become better organized, it is helpful to lead a less cluttered life. Get rid of as many possessions and activities as possible to simplify your life, and you will become more focused. Yet, your intuition might tell you that such simplification of your life might really be emotional impoverishment. You might say, "Do I really want to give up golf, my banjo collection, my shoe boxes of old family photos, and my second car just to satisfy the suggestion of this time-management specialist? My life would be much less enriched, and more boring, just to be a little more efficient in life."

Another contribution of big-picture thinking to making intelligent decisions is that it enables you to understand the point of view of others. According to Christian Knutson, a certified professional engineer, when we use big-picture thinking, we give ourselves the creative license to widen our aperture and see an issue from the perspectives of different people.[27] A plant general manager might be contemplating the decision of allowing food trucks in the plant parking lot. The permit fees would add to the profitability of the plant. In pausing to view the big picture, the general manger might think, "What will the owners of our cafeteria- catering service, and the nearby lunch services think of our decision? They have served us well for many years." Before issuing permits to outsiders, maybe we should ask the catering service and the two local restaurants if they would like to bring a food truck onto our premises."

An instructive example of looking at the big picture in making intelligent decisions is found in choosing effective locations for a business enterprise. Several important factors are the suitability of the local infrastructure, the cost of real estate, and the cost of living. The company would prefer to have suitable infrastructure in terms of such factors as adequate roads, sewers, and reasonably priced utilities. The cost of real estate can influence profitability, and the cost of living can have an impact on employee recruitment. Yet, for firms that rely heavily on the skills, talent, and educational level of employees, the availability of the needed talent in the geographic area is the big picture. Factors such as the cost of rent and utilities are more part of the little picture.

Shen Gozdan, chief financial officer of Ceniar FSB, a mortgage- servicing company, contends that it is possible to find buildings anywhere. More difficult to find, he explained, is a pool of college- educated workers who can fill customer-service roles. When Ceniar searched for a west-coast location to complement its New Jersey operations in 2015, executives invested more time analyzing labor- force data than any other factors. The company requires employees who can speak with homeowners about their mortgages, and communicate clearly by phone, e-mail, chat, and text messaging.

Ceniar looked closely at educational systems for the labor force, particularly four-year colleges with relevant majors, such as business communications, marketing, and business administration. Other relevant factors were the percentage of college graduates who remain in the geographic area, and high-quality community colleges with students who could be encouraged to earn a bachelor's degree, perhaps with tuition assistance from Ceniar. After considering cities in Arizona, Colorado, Oregon and Utah, Ceniar selected the Phoenix area. To further refine the decision, Ceniar management narrowed its decision to the city of Tempe, after outside advisors helped Ceniar develop a clearer picture of the profile of the worker it sought to attract.[28]

In short, the big picture for the mortgage-serving company was recruiting a suitable workforce. The amount of money that needs to be spent on air conditioning in Tempe was a little-picture factor.

Creating an Innovative Enterprise

Creating an innovative enterprise often requires big-picture thinking because the innovator has to imagine what else the word needs and wants. Among the many questions to ponder, are as follows:
- What could I possibly offer that would create a buzz?
- What are people looking for but they cannot find?
- What could I do to improve the lives of people that they would be willing to pay for?

A major contributor to big-picture thinking for purposes of innovation is to question traditional beliefs. A bedrock principle of both creativity and innovation is to question the way something has been done traditionally. Searching for alternatives can lead to innovation. Tradition may block potential innovations because people are reluctant to abandon what already works.[29]

In recent years, many entrepreneurs were able to spot the possibilities of the sharing economy in which people are willing to share their resources in order to earn income. A prime example is Brian Chesky, the CEO of Airbnb, a company that enables home-owners and renters of large dwellings to charge people to stay at their homes instead of renting hotel space. The big picture here is that many travelers want to pay less for lodging, dislike hotels, or a combination of the two. The innovation with respect to sharing is the companies such as

Airbnb act as digital clearing houses to enable asset owners to monetize the unused capacity of assets they already own. At the same time, consumers can rent from other people rather than rent or purchase from a company.[30]

The Airbnb experience vividly illustrates that big-picture thinking should be backed up with careful attention to details. The big picture of renters all being honest people seeking discount lodging while traveling has some merit. Yet many exceptions have emerged that force management at Airbnb to take care of some ugly details. The rare guest trashes a host's house or steals property, a situation that prompted Airbnb to carry liability insurance to reimburse hosts for damages. Other details the company has had to deal with are a variety of complications about whether Airbnb has a legal right to operate. Many codes and ordinances, for example, prohibit rentals of less than thirty days in any area other than those zoned for hotel or motel use.[31]

Next, we present two illustrations of how big-picture thinking can facilitate creating an innovative enterprise. In the first example, a traditional organization is modernized through innovative thinking.

Adapting a service to modern life. Part of a business organization being innovative is to understand what needs to be done to adapt a long- standing service to modern life. The basic service might be beneficial but needs to b tweaked to fit modern—usually digital—tastes. The big picture here is to understand how the service could fit into modern life.

Clara Shih, the CEO and co-founder of Hearsay Inc., a digital marketing software company, provides an example of a successful older company that adapted its service to the digital lifestyle. John Hancock Insurance is a traditional company whose services were marketed and provided mostly in the physical world (offline), including purchasing the policies and making claims. Also, the company has almost no contact with customers until an insured person makes a claim.

A few years ago, John Hancock formed a partnership with a small company called Vitality. The two companies launched a program where they provide free Fitbits to their policy holders for the purpose of encouraging them to be physically active, and also tracking this physical activity. John Hancock officials recognized actuarial tables indicate that the more physically active people are, the longer they live, and the healthier they are. Part of the big-picture thinking was, "Instead of being this passive assessor of risk, what if we became an active coach?"[32]

Seeing a potential borrower beyond a credit score. A small example of being an innovative enterprise by looking at the big picture is the field of microfinance. The typical microfinance company gives small loans to people who have not established a credit score, such as through previous loans. The loans are therefore made with limited data about the borrower. Shivani Siroya, the CEO of InVenture, has invented software that provides data about potential borrowers that looks a broader picture than credit score. InVenture operates in Eastern Africa,

South Africa, and India, where approximately 2.5 billion people have no credit score.

Prospective borrows download the software onto their Android smartphones. The software then monitors and crunches 10,000 indicators of the person's level of responsibility or conscientiousness. (This is the big picture about the potential borrower.) One indicator is that if the majority of a potential borrower's phone calls last more than four minutes, they are likely to have stronger relationships and be a better credit risk. For the first year in which the software was used InVenture accepted one-half the applicants for a total of more than 6,000 loans. The majority of the loans were between 20 and 100 dollars with fees, and a five percent interest rate. The repayment rate was 85 percent,[33] which was apparently good enough to enable InVenture to survive.

Being More Ethical and Socially Responsible

You are likely to conduct your work and personal life more ethically if you are a big-picture thinker. The reason is that a key contributor to being ethical is to understand how the work and other activities you are doing fit the total consequences of your actions. To take a basic example, the assistant pharmacist is behaving ethically when he or she concentrates totally on filling a prescription. To do otherwise might endanger the health of a customer by giving a person the wrong prescription or wrong dose. The big picture for a pharmacist is the welfare of patients.

R. Glenn Hubbard, dean of the Columbia Business School, believes that future leaders must connect the dots, or see the big picture, instead of focusing on their area of expertise.[34] For example, if the vice president of finance calls for reduction in expenses for new product development, the company may suffer in the long run. The unethical aspect here is that unless facing dire circumstances, cutting way back on research and development should be avoided because it presents a brighter financial picture for the present at the expense of the long-term health of the organization. Of, if the head chef uses horse meat instead of beef in certain dishes, an exposé may result that runs the restaurant out of business. (In the example of the financial vice president and the chef, the big picture is the future of the employer, and the small picture is making an immediate dollar savings.)

Corporate social responsibility is an extension of ethical behavior. It refers to the idea that firms have obligations to society beyond their financial obligations to owner. Socially responsible behavior also goes beyond those prescribed by law or contract, such as not putting toxic waste into rivers or landfills. Corporate social responsibility relates to an organization's impact on society, going beyond what doing what is ethical. A company that implemented a program of recruiting teenagers from low income families for summer jobs would be displaying corporate social responsibility. The big picture in example is that the company needs to be profitable, but it also operates in a community that needs to be financially stable. Offering teenagers summer employment adds to community stability.

Although corporate social responsibility appears to concern mostly corporate leadership, individuals throughout the organization are the building blocks of social responsibility, as well as ethical behavior. For example, a middle manager might contribute the idea of hiring a large number of teenagers for summer employment, and identify positions where they can contribute. Furthermore, the middle-manager might be assigned responsibility for the program of teenage summer employment.

Having compassion can be part of social responsibility. An exceptional example of a business leader with compassion is Father Gregory Boyle, the CDEO of Homeboy Industries. The beginning mission of the company was to create jobs for former Los Angeles gang members, many of whom had prison records. The company takes former men and women gang members and trains them in job-related skills, starting with custodial work, followed by baking skills. To create work for former gang members, Boyle started a bakery. Today the social enterprises are a bakery, Homegirl Café & Catering, Farmers Markets, Grocery, Diner, Silkscreen, and Embroidery.[35]

The Homegirl Café & Catering Enterprise helps illustrate the socially responsible nature of the enterprise started by Father Boyle. Young men and women learn got work side by side with their former enemies and gain basic job skills in a supportive environment. The café helps high risk and former gang member young women, and a few young men to become contributing members of the community through training in restaurant service and culinary arts. Homegirl Café has an 18-month training certificate program that enables women to support themselves and their families. At the same time they received needed services, such as counseling, as they work toward a better life.

Trainees cycle through three stations: café, catering, and garden and maintenance while meeting regularly with the case manager to deal with underlying needs and problems. Among these areas of assistance are mental health problems, GED preparation and testing, substance abuse, domestic violence, tattoo removal, and legal services. The trainees also attend weekly classes on life skills, restaurant operations, and café management.[36]

The big picture of Homeboy Industries is impressive, but the story also illustrates how certain details can create problems. In 2015, U.S. officials said that the Mexican mafia had united three Northeast Lost Angeles gang. The consolidated gang worked to control the local drug trade and occasionally arranged for the enemies to be killed or punished. Several of the twenty-two gang members were using Homeboy Industries to hide their criminal activities. For example, one man convicted said he one time used Homeboy Industries as a place to meet a drug dealer who owed the gang "taxes" on drug sales.

Following the arrests, Homeboy Industries issued a statement that stated in part, "As a gang rehabilitation center, we exist to support all those who want to turn away from criminal pasts and transform their lives. We understand that while we successfully help a majority of our clients, a small percentage attempt, but fail, to make that transformation."[37]

Anticipating Unintended Consequence of Your Actions

A powerful potential benefit of seeing the big picture is that it enables a person to imagine the possible negative consequences of a major decision. The law of unintended consequences states that the actions of people always have effects that are unanticipated or unintended. As originally formulated, the law applied particularly to government. For example, generous unemployment benefits are intended to help people avoid financial destruction while looking for new employment. Yet, for some people the generous benefits are an attractive alternative to working, so they scheme to receive compensation as along as possible. Economists and social scientists have been writing about and researching the law of unintended consequences for centuries.

People do not anticipate the unintended consequences of their actions and decisions for many reasons. As analyzed in 1936 by sociologist Robert K. Merton, the two most pervasive reasons for not anticipating the unintended negative consequences are ignorance and error.[38] "Ignorance" refers to having limited information, not below-average intelligence as the term is commonly used. Because it is impossible to anticipate everything, the analysis backing decision is incomplete. At one time the owner of a baseball team decided to have a free-beer night as a special promotion. The result was extensive drunk and disorderly conduct so extensive many of the families present at the ballpark were terrified. The free-beer night was never repeated. Apparently, the owner suffered from limited knowledge about how people, particularly young males, might behave on an evening out with an all-you-can-drink-for- free policy.

"Error" refers to making a mistake in analyzing the problem or following habits that worked well in the past but do not apply to the present situation. In general, safety regulations about automobiles are essential and beneficial. Passenger-side airbags were introduced in the 1990s but led to an increase in child fatalities. The unintended negative consequence was that some young children sitting in the front seat were being killed as the airbags deployed during heavy collisions. The solution to this problem was to have young (or small) children sit in the back of the vehicle in a secure child seat. Unfortunately the solution had additional dysfunctional consequences. An increase was found in the number of children forgotten in unattended vehicles, sometimes is temperatures so extreme that the occasional child asphyxiated.[39] Based on the publicity these deaths caused by negligence have received, the problem may be decreasing but still exists.

A current example of unintended negative consequence that requires big-picture thinking is the glut of cardboard boxes created by e-commerce. As Ruchit Garg, a Silicon Valley entrepreneur explains, when he opens his online shipment, he often encounters a Russian nesting doll's worth of boxes inside boxes to protect electronics, clothing, laser cartridges or groceries. The amount of containerboard to ship online purchases is increasing dramatically. Another environmental cost of all these deliveries are fleets of delivery trucks circulating in neighborhoods.

Although these unintended negative consequences of online shopping exist, there are a few counterbalancing activities. The problem of the increase in delivery truck is attenuated because online shoppers drive much less to visit physical stores. Part of the solution to the increase in corrugated packaging has been to use recycled packaging. An Amazon representative says that delivering to consumers directly from giant warehouses decreases the need to distribute to thousands of stores.[40]

A subtle example of big-picture thinking to decrease unintended negative consequences is to make major promotions from within an organization. Internal candidates are winning a high number of CEO positions at the largest American businesses. According to a recent report by the executive search firm Spencer Stuart, about four out of five major companies that chose a new CEO promoted an insider. Gregg Brenneman, an independent leader director of Home Depot Inc. says that "Developing and selecting an internal candidate seems to lead to better outcomes."[41]

Promoting an insider to chief executive helps avoid three frequently unintended consequences of bringing in an outsider. First, if the new CEO brought in from the outside fails miserably, it is an embarrassment to the company. As part of the embarrassment bringing in an outside is a costly proposition including relocation fees, a signing bonus, and paying the executive search firm. Second, bringing in an outsider often creates morale problems, and prompts many loyal employees that a policy of promotion from within does not exist. After the outsider arrives, the sentiment is often expressed, "Now we have to teach this person all about the company."

The third unintended problem is closely related to the second. Shortly after the outside CEO is hired, he or she often fires a few managers and replaces them with people from his or her former company. Many insiders despise this practice, leading to intense morale problems. A few of the more capable managers, fearing that they will be next on the hit list, quietly begin a job search.

The Downside of Big-Picture Thinking

As we have described in this chapter and will throughout the rest of the book directly or indirectly, big-picture thinking has net advantages. Nevertheless, those who paint with too broad a brush, and neglect certain realities, big-picture thinking has its limitations. The CEO of a giant multinational corporation might say during a town-hall meeting, or a meeting with investors or journalists, "We have 350,000 dedicated employees all working together to help attain our vision." The statement sounds impressive but is most likely untrue. At least ten percent of the work-force of most companies performs very poorly for reasons such as illness, low motivation, or lacking the necessary skills. Even more preposterous is the idea that 350,000 people all understand the company vision. By glossing over the realities of any problems in the workforce, the CEO is encouraging managers throughout the company not to worry about motivating and coaching employees.

Similar to the CEO is a president of the United States, or a candidate for the position, proclaiming, "We have 158 million hard working Americans (the approximate size of the workforce) trying to do better for themselves and their family." The politician loses credibility with anyone who holds a job and has observed coworkers making almost no contribution to the company. The lack of contribution to the employer takes such forms as surfing the Internet or using a smartphone for most of the day, and frequent tardiness and absenteeism. The politician in question would be more credible to more people by stating. "The vast majority of the 158 million Americans in our workforce are trying to do better for themselves and their family."

Another downside of big-picture thinking is that if uncontained it can border on hallucination. Peter Diamandis runs the X-Prize foundation that grants large cash prizes to inventors who can solve grand challenges such as space flight and oil cleanup. And Diamandis has a capacity for the broadest of big-picture thinking. He predicts that there will be 5 billion online users by 2020, perhaps double the present number of online users. "And rather than having economic shutdown, we're about to have the biggest economic injection ever. These people represent tens of trillions of dollars injected into the global economy."[42]

The hallucinatory aspect of Diamandis' thinking is his prediction about how people who go online will spend their money. Just because millions of people in impoverished, underdeveloped countries are sitting in their huts or in an igloo using a smartphone, it does not mean they will be spending their limited funds to make extensive purchases. Furthermore, sales of smartphones, tablet computers, and desktop computers had begun to level off by 2016 because the market was already saturated. A more realistic picture is that more people being online will at least stimulate the economy.

A Few Suggestions for Action

1. Recognize big-picture thinking as a most likely success factor in your career, and then take steps to view problems and opportunities in broader perspective.
2. Developing a career vision statement of about twenty-five words is .to give you a fresh and optimistic outlook on your career.
3. Carefully analyzing how your position or role fits into the big picture of your organization will help provide more meaning to what you are doing for a living.
4. Think on why the decision you are making is significant, and the long-range consequences of your decision to enhance the effectiveness of your decision.
5. To enhance your ability to innovate, attempt to question why something has been done traditionally.
6. Seeing the big-picture consequences of your actions can enhance your ability to behave ethically.
7. So many decisions have unintended consequences that it is worth your effort to visualize what could possibly go wrong with a work or personal life decision you are contemplating.

Chapter 3

The Little-Picture Thinker

Understanding the 180-degree opposite of big-picture thinking—little-picture-thinking—is helpful in developing your skills as a broad, long-range, strategic thinker. Most readers have encountered a little-picture thinker, but here is an example. Visualize a chemist who announces in the first of December that he is traveling to Stockholm, Sweden to attend a ceremony and banquet for recipients of Nobel Prize Award. His little-thinking colleague responds, "Why are you doing that? Don't you know it's very cold in Sweden in December?"

To illustrate further little-picture thinking in the midst of a big-picture event, we take the case of John Humphreys, a former marketing executive at a large lending institution. Stemming from some recent substantial organizational changes, the company had many critical issues to tackle. Among them were the following:

- Were we implementing the right competitive strategy for a newly identified target market?
- How would emerging technologies affect our company?

- How should we deal with the declining morale among our employees triggered by the company's sweeping changes?

Humphreys wrote that he was excited to be part of the group that would seek answers to these questions. Yet he was astonished, when at the first meeting with the leadership team, the discussion began with whether it was worth installing a whiteboard in a specific conference room. The next topic introduced was whether corporate office personnel should be permitted to wear denim. As part of that discussion, a meeting participant asked if chambray was a form of denim. At that point, strategically-minded Humphrey became exasperated.[43]

To get you started reflecting on your own tendencies toward little-picture thinking versus big-picture thinking, go through the accompanying checklist.

Statement in Relation to Your Thinking	Fits My Thinking
1. I would read a political editorial only if it supported my position.	
2. When someone asks me about the future, I often respond, "I don't have a crystal ball."	
3. A good way to save on money on vehicle expenses is to skip the scheduled maintenance one-half the time.	
4. I almost always refuse to consider and idea that conflicts with what I already think.	
5. I object to local, state, or provincial governments telling me not to text while driving.	
6. It is wrong that some states and provinces require people over 80 years old to take a new driver's test.	

7. I generalize a lot such as thinking that all homeless people are lazy.	
8. I avoid discussing my most important values with others because I dislike contrary arguments.	
9. Face it, most people are stupid.	
10. I complain about many things every day, including family member and conditions in the outside world.	
11. I agree that when a large, successful company hires college graduates, including MBAs, it should restrict its hiring to a few select universities.	
12. I dislike people who disagree with me about almost anything.	
13. If I did not vote for the president or prime minister of my country, I would never listen to anything he or she had to say.	
14. Several people have said that I am a poor listener.	
15. If one letter is broken on a restaurant's neon sign, I will change my plans about dining there.	

The Downside of Little-Picture Thinking

Looking at one's life and the world through a little-picture lens can block many good opportunities, as well as annoy many others. In general, being a little-picture thinker blocks a person from attaining the payoffs from big-picture thinking described in Chapter 2, including more rapid career advancement. Yet here we look at other issues stemming from the opposite of big-picture thinking.

Conflicts with big-picture thinkers. Many workplace disagreements arise because people simply dislike each other, often resulting in a personality clash. The clash reflects negative chemistry between two people. According to the research of psychologist Judith Sills, the most commonly reported office problem is the personality clash or conflict. One of the most frequent problems is between the sweeping big-picture person and the cautious detail- oriented, or little-picture person. The big-picture concert manager might say, "Give me a general idea of ticket sales for the women's soccer match," expecting a response like, "Might even fill half the seats with luck." Instead, the detail-oriented person says, "Last time I checked we had 3,578 tickets sold."

Another source of conflict is that the big-picture person is usually intuitive, and a little vague. The little-picture person is more fact- oriented and has more faith in data than personal feelings. These differences in perspectives may make each person anxious about the other.[44] A big-picture CEO of a fast-casual restaurant might say to her chief financial officer, "The fast-casual segment of the restaurant industry is hurting a little right now. Let's start a great promotion like every fourth meal is free." The little-picture CFO might say, "Let's hold off on this idea for a while. Giving away every fourth meal could eat up our profits for as long as the promotion lasts." Our little-picture chief financial officer might be right, but he has now entered into conflict with his boss. Negative career consequences, such as not receiving a year-end bonus, could result.

Overlooking good career opportunities. With a narrow perspective and little-picture thinking, a person might overlook a favorable career opportunity that does not fit a tightly-defined career plan. Or, the person might agonize over important details about the career move such as starting pay and the value of the employee benefits. A representative example of overlooking a career opportunity is that it is difficult to recruit millennials for positions in industrial sales. Although the income of sales representatives can be much higher than for other occupations open to college graduates. One problem is that selling can be risky, particularly when much of compensation is based on commission.

A study conducted by Harvard Business School found that it takes companies longer to fill technical sales jobs that other positions open to college graduates. A representative of Paycor Inc., a company that sells cloud-based software for payroll and human resource management, says that it missed out on two million more in revenue in 2015. The reason given was that the company did not meet its recruiting goals for sales representatives in the previous year.[45]

Sales executives contend that millennials, having lived through the financial crisis and then the Great Recession tend to be risk averse. Furthermore, young potential job candidates are reluctant to enter a demanding work environment where success often depends on attaining a sales quota.

Suzanne Fogel, the chair of the marketing department at the Driehaus College of Business at DePaul University provides an additional explanation for the reluctance of so many young people to enter the field of industrial sales. She says there is a strong stereotype that sales is not a true career, that either anyone can do it or you are born into the field. Many parents share the same misconceptions and dissuade their children from following a sales career path. From the standpoint of millennials, they want to be part of a team, and do not recognize that much of professional selling frequently involves working as part of a team.[46]

The big-picture look of many millennials about industrial selling is that holding a sales position is an excellent opportunity for learning about and organization, and for earning high compensation. And the biggest picture of all is that establishing a reputation as a high- performing sales representative can be a good path to the executive suite, a CEO position included. Although most CEOs worked in operations or finance, a success stint as a sales representative is still a plausible path to the top.

A study conducted by Russell Reynolds Associates (RRA), a few years ago found that firms were more likely to make CEO appointments from people with sales experience rather than finance. (RRA is a consulting firm that gathers and sells business-related information.) The reason is that firms emphasize the customer-centric nature of their businesses and want CEOs less preoccupied with investments.[47]

Little-picture thinking can sometimes block entering the sales field because they perceive such positions as selling products or services rather than also selling a purpose. Robert Matuson writes that a major reason may young people do not seek a position in sales is that the companies sell products not a purpose.[48] If the job seeker can develop the big picture of selling a purpose as well as a product or service, a position in sale might seem more desirable.

Staying in a rut. Sticking with a little picture or thinking small, can sometimes keep a person in a rut.[49] Many people stay in a job or career that brings them a minimum of satisfaction because they cannot visualize a better situation. Part of the reason for staying with an unsatisfying job can be based on worries about job security. A person who conducts a successful job search might find that the new job proves to be no more satisfying than the position abandoned. Even worse, the person might be laid off or fired from the new position, and then have to deal with the trauma of being unemployed.

Job-security concerns are certainly legitimate but harboring a little- picture viewpoint might be an equally influential factor in keeping a person in a career rut. Take the case of Quincy who has been worked as a supervisor in a machine shop for many years. He has 15 years remaining before he can retire, assuming the company stays in business and he retains his job. Quincy tolerates his role in the company but is rarely joyful about his work. Quincy looks at his career as a fixed situation that is his destiny. The thought persists, "If I can just sweat it out for fifteen more years, I will be okay."

Contrast Quincy's little-picture thinking with the big-picture thinking of Jason, a produce manager in a supermarket. Jason also is at mid-career, and he has developed an underlying uneasiness about his occupational role. Jason reasons, "There must be something else I can do with the rest of my career. The work of a produce manager is important, but I want to help people more directly. I can see myself as an ambulance medic. I would save a life on almost every shift." With this big-picture concept of a new occupational role, Jason attends a community college part-time to obtain the certification he needs to become an ambulance medic. He finds a job immediately because ambulance medics are in high demand in his community.

Jason now earns less money than he did as an experienced produce manager, but he finds more satisfaction in his new role. As a first responder, Jason gets a daily rush he never experienced in his role at the supermarket.

Micromanagement as Little-Picture Thinking

Little-picture thinking in the workplace is perhaps the most visible in the form of micromanagement. As is well known, the micromanager closely monitors most aspects of group member's activities. At his or her best, the micromanager helps make decisions about small details based on extensive technical knowledge. A micromanager of a group of clothing designers might make useful suggestions about colors, shapes, and even buttons. The suggestions aid product design, and the results are beneficial. A micromanager of a group of portfolio managers might make many useful suggestions for selecting investments that would result in better returns for the clients of the portfolio managers.

Micromanagement can also backfire because the micromanager gives subordinates limited latitude in making decisions, and makes the feel that their judgment is not trusted The micromanager takes away much of the professionalism of subordinates because he she tells them how an objective must be attained, not simply specifying what objective is required. A micromanaging sales manager might tell a sales representative, "Our goal is to increase revenues by 15 percent this quarter, and here are the ten prospects I want you to approach to hit our target." Encouraging the sales representative to choose his or her own prospects would reflect less micromanagement.

Micromanagers often neglect the big picture because they focus so much on details that they overlook the general purpose of what group members are attempting to achieve. A police captain might be making a PowerPoint presentation on how to reduce violent crime in her district. While watching the presentation, the micromanaging chief of police makes several suggestions about the background and fonts used on the slides, yet he asks no questions about the topic of reducing crime.

A micromanager is also referred to as a control freak because he or she wants to maintain so much control. Mickey Drexler, formerly of Gap, and newly retired CEO and Chairman of the Board of J. Crew, is by his own admission a control freak. His job satisfaction is the highest when he is involved in every facet of merchandising, even button selection. He also personally responds to shopper e-mails and phone calls.

Drexler was the head of a successful large business enterprise, so he qualifies as a big-picture thinker who also has little-picture tendencies. He appears to use little pictures to help build the big picture. Drexler recently asked customers to visit his stores and check out the e-commerce site to see how J. Crew had returned to its former glory. He also posted his e-mail address, and asked customers to e-mail him directly with their thoughts.[50]

Drexler is an acknowledged merchandising talent, and also CEO and part owner of J. Crew, so his micromanaging style is tolerated. At a team or department level, a micromanager might be perceived as more of an annoyance.

Micromanagement has some potential benefits, such as enhancing the creative contribution of the manager and providing close guidance to the person being managed. Nevertheless, micromanagement it usually involves little-picture thinking, as shown in in following manifestations:

- The company CEO signs all checks or authorizes online payments over $300 other than paychecks.
- The manager insists that her favorite two fonts be used on all official company communications.
- The manager frequently hears the comment from subordinates, "Why are you looking over my shoulder so often?"
- The CEO has a long series of e-mail exchanges with the HR head, reviewing what types of food and beverages should be served at the year-end party. Furthermore, the CEO arranges for a meeting with the manager of the restaurant chosen to discuss planning for the party.
- The manager insists on fact checking any report to be sent from her department.

- The division general manager establishes a time-recording system to be used by every employee in the division, from entry-level workers to department heads.
- The manager asks the vending-machine supplier for a report on the nutritional value of each food and beverage offered in the vending machines used by the company.
- The manager asks the employees in the department to keep a daily time log of their activities each working day, and to submit the time log to him each week.
- The manager distributes an e-mail to employees a list of restaurants that she thinks offer healthy enough cuisine to be eaten at lunch.
- An office supervisor spots an administrative assistant using a coffee mug decorated with the face of a clown. She suggests to the user of this mug that he "Find a more professional looking coffee mug."

Polite confrontation can be helpful in dealing with a micromanager. If you feel that you are being supervised so closely that it is difficult to perform well, confront the situation in a non-hostile, non-aggressive way. Say something of this nature: "I notice that you check almost all my work. Do you doubt my ability to perform my job correctly?"

Another useful question might be, "What can I do to show you that I can work well independently?" As a consequence, your manager might explain why he or she is micromanaging or begin to check you work less frequently.

The Silo Mentality and Little-Picture Thinking

As you drive past farms, factories, and refineries it is easy to recognize those high and wide vertical structures resembling large tubes. They are referred to as silos and serve the important purpose of bulk storage of various commodities. Despite the importance of silos to farming, mining, and industry, they have developed a bad rap in the office. A *silo mentality* (or *silo mindset*) refers to a situation in which people of one group feel competitive with other groups to the extent that cooperation suffers. The physical analogy is that a silo stands independently without interacting with other structures.

Part of the silo mentality is understandable because it is natural to devote your primary attention to the organizational unit in which your work. As business writer Neil Smith explains, managers tend to look up and down their own silo without looking around or across. As a result, all they see and tend to think about is their own silos. Furthermore, they have limited knowledge about what is happening elsewhere in the organization or how their actions affect those in other organizational units.[51]

The silo mentality also refers to the idea that people in one group do not want to share information with others in the same company. Instead of seeing the big picture of sharing information across organizational units, they see the little picture of hogging information and other resources. People with a silo mentality have very little interest in the success of the organization as a whole. Take this scenario of little-picture thinking that reflects a silo mentality:

Package designers in one unit of a large pharmaceutical company develop an easy-to-open plastic container that would avoid unintentional opening but would still be easy to manipulate for people with weak fingers or hands. People suffering from arthritis and other joint diseases would find the container particularly useful. The new package design might prove useful to other to other divisions of the pharmaceutical company. However, the head of the unit in question says, "Why share our design with other units who sell packaged over-the-counter drugs? We will get much more credit if we can hang onto this design for ourselves as long as possible."

The contrast to the silo (or little-picture) mentality in this situation would be, "We are on to something that will help many units in our firm market their products better. We can also decrease aggravation for thousands of customers who have weak hands and fingers. Let's broadcast our discovery starting later today."

Another aspect of little-picture thinking with respect to a silo mentality is that collaboration will be limited unless collaboration benefits the members of the organizational unit (the silo). The little-picture perspective is reinforced because members of the silo tend to think alike. This is true partially because the silo members derive their power from association with their organization function, and their shared job knowledge.[52]

Another frame for understanding the little-picture nature of silos, is that the silo mentality has been referred to as departmental politics, divisional rivalry, or turf warfare.

According to consultant Bruce Holland, it is not only the organizational structure that brings about the silo effect, it is the thinking of people[53]. In other words, if people can overcome little-picture thinking, the silos might dissolve.

The silo mentality about recruiting, developing, and retaining employees. The field of human resource management presents an informative example of how a silo mentality might deter an organization from making the best use of its talent. According to Michael E. Echols, the vice president of strategic initiatives at Bellevue University, many professional workers quit their employer because they see no attractive career path in the company. Echols believes that the talent needed to compete in the rapidly changing world is becoming more difficult to find and retain.

To do a better job of finding and retaining talent, the functions of recruiting, developing, and retaining workers have to overcome working in silos. In the typical approach, the recruiting and selection function uses a variety of recruiting tools, interviews, and hires new employees. The learning function trains and develops employees after they are hired. Managers in other departments are responsible for retaining employees.

Instead of operating in silos, Echols recommends that the learning (or training and development) function can help in recruiting. The reason is that many professional and technical workers are attracted to organizations that offer the prospects of professional development, such as coaching and continuing education. The learning function can also enhance retention for the same reason. Professional and technical workers are more inclined to stay with a company that offers them career-related learning.

Providing good learning opportunities to current employees also helps in recruiting because employees who upgrade their skills can fill positions in the company where such skills are needed. A big-picture perspective is that for many positions employers should look beyond potential external candidates with a college degree. The extended approach is to develop those already inside the organization who do not have a college degree but demonstrate a commitment to learn. One interpretation of the current labor market is that for the next decade there will not be enough external candidates available with the needed credentials for companies to recruit.[54]

Creating visibility for projects to overcome the silo mentality. If workers within self-contained functions, or silos, are more aware of projects going on in the organization, the chances increase of seeing the big picture. Human Resources consultant, Ingrid Cliff recommends increasing the visibility of projects so that many people will look outside their silos. These awareness raisers could include dissemination of information about projects on company intranets or a simple white-board list. Whatever system is used needs to be regularly updated. To avoid confusing people, only one version of the project announcement should be used. The information about the project should be visible to all people who have an interest.[55]

Assume that the finance department within a company is starting a project to hold a garage sale of unwanted, redundant, or obsolete equipment in order to improve the company's cash flow. If this modest project is publicized on a company social media site, many managers and other workers might peer out over their silos and volunteer to contribute some items for sale.

Breaking the silo barrier sensibly. Silos are a natural phenomenon when an organization is divided into departments. Theorists and researchers about organizations have been proposing for a long time that the department structure be replaced by a more free-flowing structure in which workers focus more on the customer. In reality, this suggestion is naïve, and the most vocal critics of department structures want such a structure when faced with an urgent personal need, as illustrated in the following scenario:

A well-respected and well-known business strategy professor at Harvard Business School has suggested for years that the field of medicine must replace department and functional structures. The replacement he suggests is some kind of amorphous structure that focuses on value to the patient, not the convenience of medical professionals. One day our professor is driving his car with a passenger in the front seat. Unfortunately, the vehicle bangs into a truck in front of the professor and his passenger. The passenger is bleeding from a wound in the forehead even though the airbag deployed.

Without waiting to deal with the police and the truck driver for now, the professor heads for the hospital and wheels toward a sign that says, "Emergency Care." For the moment, the professor has forgotten about his disdain for departments in hospital. He intuitively knows that having a specialized department for urgent care makes sense and could be life-saving.

Common sense suggests that you visit the emergency department when you have a medical emergency. At emergency care you are likely to find specialists who can help you. Wouldn't this be better than a hospital with no departments, just a giant collection of care providers who also dealt with pediatrics, OBGYN, intensive care, and so forth?

The point here is that it may be important to reduce the little-picture thinking of the silo mentality, but it makes sense to keep the silos. Without silos, we would have too many generalists and too few specialists, such as accountants, grouped together to deal with company accounting.

According to Neil Smith, the general solution for the problem stemming from a silo mindset is being able to look and understand things from a different person's or department's viewpoint. The software specialist assigned to a smartphone project would be taking this viewpoint when she thinks, "I know that I am going to wow my colleagues when I make these ten changes in the software for the next version of our phone. But I could be creating problems for marketing and sales and our dealers. We would have a lot of people attempting to return our phones in disgust because the new features are so confusing to the ordinary user."

Another deep-rooted problem creating the silo mentality is that human nature prompts people to want to do the best they can within their own sandbox, at the expense of other people. A feeling of ownership about a function or department fosters a manager's entrepreneurial spirit. The manager's rationalization for poor cooperation with other units is "I've been given this are to run as I see fit, and I need to do the best job I possibly can."

Given that the reasons for a silo mentality, and its associated little-picture thinking, are so deep, it may take some serious thinking to develop a broader perspective. Neil Smith has developed five provocative questions that the heads of organization units might ask to transcend the silo mentality:[56]

1. Which priorities of yours or your department do not align with those of other managers and departments?

2. What would make another silo understand that your need was a priority?

3. What information do you or your department have that could be useful to others in the organization?

4. What information or assistance do you need from another organizational unit (silo) that you are not receiving?

5. In what areas would an increase in collaboration and surrendering a little autonomy be more beneficial for the company than maintaining your individuality?

Perhaps these questions would make for useful dialogue within the department. Even just asking these questions would sensitive the managers and other members of the department to the need to overcome the silo mentality and move on to big-picture thinking.

Narrow Mindedness and Little-Picture Thinking

Narrow-minded is an adjective with two frequently-used meanings, with both being linked to seeing the little picture. One meaning has to do with having or showing a prejudiced mind or being biased. An employment recruiter might be biased against liberal arts graduates thinking that they are too idealistic, dislike capitalism, and have a weak work ethic. This narrow-mind perception of liberal arts graduates might block the recruiter from taking a broader perspective that many successful people in business, including entrepreneurs and CEOs were liberal arts graduates.

Narrow-minded ness also refers to not being receptive to new ideas or having a closed-mind. This meaning of narrow-mindedness points directly to having a little-picture perspective because the person does not take the broader view that other viewpoints are possible. A narrow-minded person might think, "I will not purchase any clothing for myself online. If I cannot try on clothing or touch it before making a purchase, I will not buy that item." Yet, with a broader point of view, perhaps purchasing loose-fitting sweater online, the person might discover that online shopping for clothing has some merits. He or she might save some time, save on the cost of driving a vehicle, and deliver fewer pollutants to the air caused by driving a vehicle.

We chose the concept of narrow-mindedness rather than small-mindedness in our discussion of seeing the little picture although the latter could still be relevant. A small-minded person is considered to be petty or selfish, so he or she could miss out on the big picture of treating other people well to form better interpersonal relationships.

A man met a woman online, and the two arranged to meet at a moderately-priced restaurant. To the man's surprise, the woman was even more attractive in the real than virtual world. When it came time to order the main meal, he suggested that they share one meal that would pay for. The woman was so negatively impressed by the man that she basically ignored him during the meal and exited the situation at the earliest polite moment. The man's small-mindedness with respect to buying a separate meal for the woman choked off the possibility of getting another date with her. (A different take on this scenario, is that the woman was being narrow-minded by not overlooking the man's small-mindedness!)

A person who wanted to change from being narrow minded to broad minded would have already taken an important first step. Most narrow minded people do not recognize that they are narrow minded or perceived by others to be narrow minded. Recognizing that change is desirable is therefore a key starting point. Another difficulty in changing from being narrow minded to broad minded, is that the perspective is often based on values and personality traits.

Values influence being narrow minded because they determine what a person considers to be acceptable behavior, and this is difficult to change. Baxter has a strong work ethic so he might believe that a physically-abled adult should strive to find work rather than be dependent on the family, the government, or strangers to help him or her financially. One day

Baxter is downtown and is approached by a man who appears to be in is mid-twenties, and in good physical condition. He says to Baxter in aggressive tone, "Can you spare me some change? I'm hungry." Baxter has immediate disdain for the stranger, and says, "Get out of here, and go find a job."

Some people might agree with Baxter, but others might think he is being narrow minded. He is unwilling to think of possible reasons why this man is in need of money for food. Among these explanations could be that the man (a) is mentally ill, (b) was part of a corporate downsizing, (c) went bankrupt because of medical expenses, or (d) spent all his money helping family members.

Personality traits are another major influence on whether or not a person is narrow minded. Natalie has a very high standing on the trait of perfectionism, so from her point of view things must be just right for her to find them acceptable. Today Natalie is at an animal shelter to adopt a cat because her beloved cat of fifteen years died two weeks ago. Her life feels empty without being a cat owner. At the shelter she sees a tiger kitten of about six weeks old. Natalie adores tiger cats, and the kitten yawns in front of her. The immediate chemistry is strong, and Natalie is all set to be her adoptive owner. Then Natalie notices that one of the kitten's paws is completely white, whereas the other four are the same natural tiger pattern as her body. Natalie nixes the adoption with the thought, "Lovable kitten, but I don't want a cat with an obvious flaw."

Some people might perceive Natalie to be narrow minded because she turned down adopting a kitten for a petty reason.

Yet other people might say that Natalie is being realistic. Why adopt a cat that you intend to keep for his or her life if it has a flaw that bothers you? There are a lot of other cats up for adoption.

The following suggestions should prove useful in making the journey from having a narrow-minded, little-picture perspective, the a broader-minded, big-picture perspective:[57]

- When faced with a situation calling for your interpretation of what is happening, ask yourself, "What would be the narrow perspective here?" and "What would be the broad perspective here?" For example, if a supervisor notices that a worker arrives at the office looking disheveled one interpretation might be that the worker is unprofessional. Another interpretation might be that this is a one-time event, most likely reflecting the reality that the person is experiencing a problem this morning.

- Attempt to minimize broad generalizations when making a judgment about a person's most probable behavior or attitude. A recurring example is the generalization that workers with exceptional technical skills would not be interested in a position involving extensive contact with people. In reality, the majority of successful leaders used advanced technical skill as the foundation of their career. One such person is Alan Mulally, the former highly successful CEO of Ford Motor Company. In his early days at Boeing Inc., he distinguished himself as an aeronautical engineer.

- Socialize with a wider variety of people. A prevalent characteristic of narrow-minded people is that they find a variety of reasons not to socialize with other people. Among the reasons for rejecting others are disagreeing with their political beliefs, thinking they are stupid, or deeming them to be of lower class. Making the effort to socialize with a broader range of people can broaden one's outlook.
- Look for positives as well as negatives in people and situations. Many people never follow the news with the excuse that "Almost all the news is negative." Even if this perception has some truth, being uninformed is a swift path to narrow-mindedness. Continuous complaining about your employer can also facilitate narrow-mindedness and little-picture thinking because a person excludes the possibility that something might be beneficial. A person might complain about company leadership spending money to purchase another company. The complaint blocks out the positive thought that as a result of the acquisition, the company might become stronger and more promotional opportunities for might be forthcoming.
- Be open to new ideas. A defining characteristic of a narrow- minded person is blocking out new opinions and ideas, even when the new opinions and ideas have demonstrated validity. An administrative assistant at an enterprise software company heard that the company was going to hire a few autistic people as software engineers as "a crazy idea". She did not listen to the newly-found reality that many autistic people have strong powers of concentration that facilitate their being able to find coding errors.

- Listen more carefully. It is easy to stay narrow minded when a person waits for the opportunity to talk without listening to a differing opinion. You can see this pattern of behavior with a television newscaster who invites a person with a completely different point of view to be a guest on the show. When the guest attempts to explain his or her point of view, the host interrupts and talks over the person, while repeating his or her viewpoint that differs from the guest.

A Few Suggestions for Action

1. Minimize being a little-picture thinker to the exclusion of occasionally being a big-picture thinker. As you focus on the necessary details of a task or situation, pause to think, "What is the big picture here that I should also be thinking of?"

2. When contemplating a new position, or perhaps entry into a new field, look broadly at possible opportunities rather than staying with a narrow conception of a suitable new position.

3. If you contact with little-picture thinking takes the form of being micromanaged, confront your micromanager in a constructive, non- hostile way to attain more latitude in your performing you job.

4. A silo mentality may be natural, particularly if you are a talented specialist. To soften your silo mentality, pause to thinking how others outside your organizational unit are using your output, and how you can work more cooperatively and collaboratively with them.

5. To help overcome tendencies toward narrow-minded oneself; it is useful to challenge standard beliefs about people and situations. For example: A person might decide not to play golf because it takes so long to play. In reality, many golf clubs allow for playing a course with fewer holes.

Chapter 4

Characteristics of Big-Picture Thinkers

In recent years, young people have started to unleash the economic promise of the prominent manufacturing cities of the past, particularly, Detroit, Cleveland, Baltimore, and Pittsburgh. Youthful entrepreneurs see the opportunity to create new enterprises in these cities where lower barriers to starting a business exist. "Right now in Detroit, it's cheaper to fail," says Jay Rayford, who runs a networking group that connects people of different backgrounds and social segments. City leaders see enticing professional, innovative types who drive growth and profits as a key to triggering a Rustbelt renaissance.[58] A major attribute of these Millennials share is big-picture thinking about the possibilities of revitalizing these cities to their former glory days.

Although we have already described many attributes of big-picture thinkers, more details are warranted for two major reasons. Suppose you want to become a big-picture thinker because of many of its perceived benefits such as better upward mobility in your career. As a consequence it would be helpful to examine closely the cognitive makeup of such people. Knowing these characteristics can give you a few hooks to work with in terms of personal development. For example, if you become aware that big-picture thinkers habitually gather ideas from others, you can develop this approach without having to change your personality traits.

Another reason for understanding the characteristics of big-picture thinkers is that it enables you to work better with them. For instance, one of the characteristics of a big-picture thinker described in this chapter is passion for the work or task. Recognizing this characteristic will make it easy to understand why a big thinker in your network is so exuberant about what you might regard as an ordinary work assignment.

Focus on Ideas More than Facts

A dominant characteristic of big-picture thinkers is that they emphasize ideas and concepts rather than facts or details. The term emphasize is important here, because an effective big-picture thinker favors looking at the big-picture but does not totally neglect or ignore details. At a public meeting a big-picture-thinking mayor might say, "Our goal for the next year is to practically eliminate homelessness. No longer will we have our society's most unfortunate people freezing to death in cold weather and broiling to death under extreme heat. We will have loads of dormitories for the homeless the way they do in Salt Lake City."

Following mention of this general humanitarian plan, the mayor makes no mention of such facts as (a) who will pay for the dormitories, (b) where they will be located, (c) how homeless people will be enticed or coerced into moving into the dormitories, and (d) for how long a period of time will a person be able to stay in a dormitory. Perhaps the big-picture-thinking mayor will provide details in a later meeting or have someone else from the mayor's office provide the key facts.

Idea-focused people prefer concepts to a long list of details. If you are idea-focused you are more likely to focus on the future than the present, as in presenting a vision to your listeners. As explained by leadership coach Denise Brouillette, the idea-focused person recognizes that taking risks can result in big payoffs.[59] The idea-focused CEO might say, "If we invest three million in a solar-panel farm now, we might be able to reduce our electricity costs by 50 percent in four years."

The idea-focused individual will often have to back up his or her ideas with facts in order to convince fact-focused people. Our solar-panel enthusiast would do well to present some hard data about the return on investment stemming from these panels.

A preference for ideas rather than fact also takes the form of thinking in broad strokes rather than detail, much like a house painter painting a wall rather than the trim on a window. While negotiating with the top-level management of a restaurant chain, the negotiator representing entry-level workers might first work in broad strokes. She begins her demands asking for "wages and benefits that will enable our beginning workers to support their families and lead a decent life." She keeps hammering at this broad-stroke demand to help sensitize restaurant leadership to the fact that entry-level restaurant workers must be paid generously. The broad-stroke demand often works, but our negotiator must soon get to the details of what she really wants to gain much for her side. Again, the big-picture is a fine starting point, but it must eventually be supported by workable details.

Another way in which the focus on ideas rather than details manifests itself is the ability to see the big-picture rather than getting lost in the details. As analyzed by Mike Adams, an editor at Natural News, many people with high intelligence cannot see the big-picture because they get lost in the details. He writes that "it is not uncommon to see a high-level mathematics professor with an IQ of 175 chowing down on a processed hamburger laced with toxic chemical additives, while wearing clothes washed in carcinogenic mainstream laundry detergent."[60] The big picture, or general idea, that Adams wants the professor to see is the presence of toxic chemicals in his or her daily life. Instead, the mathematics professor is focused on the details of advanced mathematics. (The analogy Adams makes is useful here, but we doubt he really measured the IQ of the professors to whom he referred.)

Assimilating large numbers of details can lead to thinking in terms of ideas, and the putting the details aside. This pattern of thinking is referred to as the ability to "connect the dots." A flight attendant might see large number of tall passengers either bumping their head as they enter or exit the plane or ducking down. She then develops the big idea of recommending to management that when new airplanes are purchased, they should be at least six inches higher within the cabin.

Personality Factor of Openness to Experience

Personality traits exert a strong influence on virtually all aspects of human behavior, so it is not surprising that a trait can partially govern a person's tendency toward being a big-picture thinker. A factor in this context is a cluster of traits. Openness to experience is much like intellectual curiosity and is linked consistently to creativity.

Research by psychologist and human-mind specialist Scott Barry Kaufman revealed that there are four components associated with openness to experience.[61] Each one of these components provides clues to why a person who is high on openness to experience would tend toward being a big-picture thinker.

1. *Explicit cognitive ability.* The reference here is to traditional intelligence, such as that associated with high scholastic achievement and solving difficult problems. If you are intellectually bright it is easier to create visions and other scenarios that become part of the big picture. For example, visualizing the Hyperloop described in Chapter 1 required substantial high-level cognitive ability.

2. *Intellectual engagement.* The core of this component is a drive to engage in ideas, rational thought, and the search for truth. People scoring high on this component tend to be more industrious, assertive, and persevering—and therefore more likely to pursue goals. The pursuit of the big-picture requires

such goal-directed behavior. A big-picture thinking chemist might think, "My team and I will not give up until we find a financially feasible way of desalinizing water. We have states and countries adjacent to ocean water, yet people, animals and land are starving for water. I know that we will conquer this dreadful problem plaguing our planet."

3. *Affective engagement.* The essence of this component is a preference for relying on emotions, gut feelings, and empathy to solve problems and make decisions. People who score high on affective engagement tend to be more volatile, compassionate, enthusiastic, assertive, and impulsive. Visualizing the big-picture is an act that requires considerable emotion and intuition. (More about this will be presented later in the chapter.) The big-picture-thinking chemist just mentioned is emotional about people and animals suffering from malnutrition and dehydration, yet with an ocean nearby.

4. *Aesthetic engagement.* The core ingredient of this factor is a preference for aesthetics, fantasy, and emotional absorption in artistic and cultural activities. A common theme of this component is a search for beauty. The late Steve Jobs who cofounded Apple Inc. was a big-picture thinker who was focused strongly on the beauty of the products he helped create, such as desktop computers and smartphones. At the same time Jobs was a little-picture thinker who would throw temper tantrums and publicly berate others if he disliked a small design detail.

Gaining Insights from a Variety of People

The personality trait of openness to experience facilitates a big-picture thinker gaining insights from a variety of people. John C. Maxwell, author of *How Successful People Think*, writes that big-picture thinkers gain insights from many people including customers, employees, coworkers, and company leaders.[62] Although true that big-picture thinkers are bright and creative, systematically gathering input from others helps they develop a broad perspective.

Gaining insights from many people is also referred to as paying attention to stakeholders—all those people who have a stake in the organization. As a result, a lot of people have to be listened to, both internal and external stakeholders. Assume that Gloria, the CEO and chairperson of a large discount retailer has a high standing on openness to experience. The company has physical stores throughout the world, and also sells some merchandise online. Although the chain is remarkably successful, Gloria likes to hone her big picture of the enterprise She therefore gathers input from the four internal stakeholders and eight external stakeholders. Snippets of their input that lead to a big-picture for the CEO are provided next.

Internal Stakeholders
- The owners tell Gloria that all is going well, but that she should be careful not to move the chain out of its category and become a low-quality discounter or a traditional department store.
- The stockholders are satisfied, but during a company meeting many of them expressed in interest in receiving more

frequent and higher dividends. They would also like to see the stock price move up more consistently.

- The employees generally enjoy working for the company, as reflected in lower turnover in terms of industry averages. Yet they would like higher hourly pay, and more predictable work schedules.
- The board of directors like what they see but want to learn more about Gloria's strategy for growth and survival in an era when physical retail stores are in decline. The board is also worried about the major traditional retailers setting up their own discount stores or discount departments.

External Stakeholders

- The customers remain king and queen for any retail executive including Gloria. She carefully monitors e-mails sent to the company as well as social media posts, and direct comments made to the customer service department in the stores. Gloria hears that customers love the "treasure hunt" aspect of the store, and the fact that prices for such high-quality merchandise are usually low. Yet Gloria also notes that many customers do not like how merchandise is strewn across the floor in some departments by customers.
- The suppliers are a happy lot, particularly now that many of them ship clothing directly from their factory to store locations. Suppliers who sell their excess and out-of-season merchandise to the store would like to receive payments more quickly.

- The creditors are few in number because the company usually has enough cash flow to avoid borrowing money. The few creditors that exist are happy because the company pays back its loans promptly.
- The competitors have mixed feelings about the company. The success of Gloria's company has enlarged the category for a high-quality discount store. Affluent people are included among is shoppers, and this category does well during a recession as well as during prosperous times.
- Special interest groups present few problems for this retail chain. For example, the company does not sell real furs so groups aimed at ethical treatment of animals are not upset. Furthermore, the company has not been accused of purchasing from suppliers that use child labor, and the stores create no obvious environmental problems.
- Consumer groups have not voiced complaints against the retailer because these groups usually focus their complaints against manufacturers of unsafe devices such as faulty airbags, dangerous cribs, and hoverboards. (A hoverboard is a battery-powered scooter that requires no steering bar.) The vast majority of the merchandise sold by the company is in the clothing category, thereby escaping almost all safety recalls.
- Government agencies appear to like the retailer because it has so few problems such as safety violations or large numbers of complaints about sexual harassment. Furthermore, the company hires large numbers of customer-contact workers and managers who are minorities. The company also reaches out to

physically handicapped people to find suitable employment for them.
- Financial institutions generally like the chain but would like to see more steady growth in stock price. Yet Gloria resists maneuvers to cut costs, such as closing the poorest performing stores, just to boost the stock price. She says proudly, "The stock price is not the company."

Carefully absorbing all this input, Gloria continues to present the big-picture of a large retail chain that offers customers designer and name brand labels at deep discounts.

Gloria believes that the chain has found the right category or niche and will continue to occupy the same retail space. She also talks about a store that is in the forefront of being an equal-opportunity employer, and cares about profits but is not obsessed with cost cutting or maximizing the stock price. In discussions with her management team, Gloria includes such little-picture items as working on the problem of having merchandise strewn on the floor and thrown on top of clothing racks.

Divergent Thinking

Divergent, or *lateral*, thinking has long been recognized as a way of arriving at creative thoughts. Divergent thinking spreads out to find many alternative solutions to a problem. Vertical thinking is an analytical, logical process that results in few answers. In contrast, creative thinking is lateral. A vertical thinker might say, "I must find a part-time job to supplement my income. My income is not matching my expenses." The lateral thinker might say, "I need more money. Let me think of various ways or earning or having more money. I can find a second job, get promoted where I am working, cut my expenses, run a small business out of my home . . ."

Big-picture thinking emphasizes divergent thinking because the search for broad, visionary ideas involves considerable creativity. A local artisan might be making decorative smartphone cases that are selling well from her kiosk located in a mall. She is eking out a living, but then starts thinking divergently: "Where else might my smartphone cases fit into the world? I know there is competition, but our decorations are unique." Her divergent thinking then slides into seeing the big-picture. A new thought emerges: "Practically two-thirds of the people in the world own smartphones. Many of these people are fashion conscious. Maybe I could find distributors and manufacturers in Europe, Asia, and Africa who would work with me to penetrate markets throughout the world."

Divergent thinking also takes the form of thinking broadly. Leadership professor James G. Clawson writes that members in less bureaucratic organizations need to develop broader ways of thinking about their work. No longer can they say, "That's not my job," and expect they can hold onto their jobs or that their employer will survive.[63]

Managers and individual contributors alike have to recognize that every employee has something to contribute that extends outside their job description.

The thoughts just expressed point to the idea that in a modern organization, many more people need to see the big-picture. An assembly worker at a bicycle factory might, "Two of my granddaughters told me that they want a purple bike, and so do their friends. Maybe it's time for our company to stop building so many pink bikes for girls." An information technology technician in the accounting office might engage in big-picture thinking by sending an e-mail of this nature to top management: "Our company doesn't appear to be getting it from a green standpoint. We need to show the world that we are environmentally friendly. We should plant a few rooftop gardens, and charter a few park-and-ride buses to show the world we care about the environment."

Intuitive Problem-Solving Style

In Chapter 2 we describe intuition as part of making intelligent decisions. It follows naturally that intuitive problem solving is characteristic of big-picture thinkers. People who rely heavily on intuition in problem solving look for patterns and interrelationships. Intuitive people also focus on the big-picture or broad issues. According to the still widely-used Meyers-Briggs Type Indicator, people who rely on intuition tend to take in information by seeing the big-picture. They focus on the relationships and connections among facts. Intuitive types want to grasp patterns and are open to new possibilities.[64] The accompanying self-quiz provides you an opportunity to measure your tendencies toward being an intuitive problem solver and decision maker.

The Intuitive Problem-Solving Style Quiz

Indicate your strength of agreement with each of the following statements: SD - strongly disagree; D – disagree; N – neutral, A – agree; SA – strongly agree.

	SD	D	N	A	SA
1. Most of my hunches prove to be correct.	1	2	3	4	5
2. Details tend to take care of themselves providing you are on the right track with your plans.	1	2	3	4	5
3 Before attempting to solve a problem, I gather a large number of relevant fact.	5	4	3	2	1
4 Relying on gut feel is a terrible way for a business executive to decide.	5	4	3	2	1
5. When I meet a person for the first time, I take my time in deciding whether he or she and I will get along.	5	4	3	2	1
6. It takes me about ten seconds to know if I am physically attracted to another person. (Skip this question if you are in a committed relationship.) ☺	1	2	3	4	5
7. It takes me a long time to decide whether I like the color on a vehicle I am thinking about purchasing.	5	4	3	2	1
8. I need, or would need, to gather a lot of facts before I would purchase stock in a specific company.	5	4	3	2	1
9. When making an important decision, it is much better to gather new facts rather than rely on past experience.	5	4	3	2	1

10. Common sense is an effective source of information for making decisions.	1	2	3	4	5
11. I usually "jump to a conclusion" when making a decision.	1	2	3	4	5

Scoring and interpretation: Find your total score by summing the point values for each question.

65 – 75: You probably have a strong intuitive decision-making style that facilitates being a big-picture thinker.

36 – 60: You probably have a balanced approach between an intuitive decision-making style and one that relies more on facts and research.

15 – 35: Your decision-making style probably emphasizes basing your decisions on facts and careful observation rather than on intuition.

Entrepreneurial big-picture thinking and intuition. Entrepreneurs are often big-picture thinkers because they have to envision the possibilities of an enterprise starting from a basic idea. The sharing economy was in large part started by entrepreneurs who had a basic idea for people sharing goods or services, and then built an enterprise starting from scratch. The colonel idea was to take something that already existed on a small scale and expand it into a large business. For example, people had shared automobiles, given strangers auto rides for a few dollars, and rented their homes to strangers for many years. Eventually these activities became nationwide businesses.

Katherine Long of Illustria Designs represents a specific example of how an entrepreneur uses intuition to help see the big-picture. Long is a graduate of the Wharton School of the University of Pennsylvania. She began her marketing design company in 2013, immediately after obtaining her MBA. Illustria provides high quality, moderately priced, designs for logos, websites, mobile apps and other marketing materials.

Long's formal business education gave her good insight into quantitative-decision making tools, such as making forecasts with spreadsheets. Yet she was also aware that creativity and insight contribute to thinking of an idea for a new business. So she relied on her intuition to tell her that a need existed for low-cost marketing designs.

"That's typically how it happens for entrepreneurs," says Long. "You experience a problem and you figure out how to solve it. You have to be in touch with your intuition and creativity because it's not often something can reason your way into with data."[65] Illustria has become a successful enterprise built on Long using her intuition to see the big-picture of how affordable designs for marketing could fit into the world.

Kristin Smith, the CEO of Code Fellows, a software programming school, also feels strongly about how intuition contributes to entrepreneurship. She says that the entrepreneur cannot rely on logic and formulas alone. He or she has to conduct real-world research and listen and learn. The listening and learning provides the raw data for intuition.[66] (Listening to customers, as in focus groups, is a standard marketing technique.)

Using both Hemispheres of the Brain to Produce Intuition. Conventional wisdom is that people learn and acquire information in one of two ways, relying heavily on different parts of the brain. Some learners are "right brained," showing a preference to learn and process information simultaneously. They tend to focus on the big-picture and the relationships between ideas, leading to higher creativity. Other people tend to be "left brain," and learn and process information in a sequential, step-by-step fashion, and focus on details. As a result these people are more logical and analytical.[67]

The popular belief is therefore that creative people are right-brain dominant, whereas left-brain dominant people are more logical, detail oriented, and analytical. However, this belief has been challenged in recent years by brain specialists. Current neuroscience research suggests that developing original ideas is a process, and not something that stems from one aside of the brain. Antonio Damasio, director of the Brain and Creativity Institute at the University of Southern California, explains that there is a high level of cooperation between different parts and different systems within the brain.[68]

As a result, creative problem-solving, and intuition are orchestrated by different parts of the brain working together. The imagination that is an integral part of creativity and intuition stems from memory because memory is essential to recognized when something is original—a key component of creativity.

Both sides of the brain are also needed for learning. Just as people need to see with both eyes to capture all of the nuances of an image, the two halves of the brain are needed for learning. People need to gather information from both the "big-picture" and "detail" perspectives in order to fully understand what they are learning.[69] The link to intuition is that people are more intuitive when they have learned a lot in the past.

The implication for people who want to fine-tune their brains so they can be more intuitive and better at seeing the big-picture is to develop both sides of the brain. Continue to gather facts and store them in your brain so you have the raw material for creativity. This is particularly true because creativity often consists of combining facts that were not combined previously. For example, a digital camera is a combination of the essential features of a film camera and a small computer. In addition to working the left side of the brain, it is helpful to refine the right side of the brain by engaging in creative activities such as drawing, painting, making up jokes, and writing poems. When both sides of the brain are working smoothly, you are more likely to become an intuitive thinker who can see the big picture.

Passion for the Work or Task

Big-picture thinkers, similar to entrepreneurs and effective leaders in business, government, and education tend to be passionate about what their professional responsibilities. Passion for the work or task will often prompt a person to look for the broader significance of what he or she is doing. An accounts payable specialist at a building-supply company might think, "Collecting the money we are owed from our customers is no ordinary task. If we don' get our money, we can't pay our employees or our suppliers. Then our company would collapse."

A dominant characteristic of creative people—who are often big-picture thinkers—is passion for the work. More than twenty years of research conducted in industry by Teresa M. Amabile and her associates led to the internal motivation principle of creativity. People will be at their creative best when they feel motivated primarily by the interest, satisfaction, and challenge of the work itself, and not by external pressures.[70]

Quite similar to creative people, a strong characteristic of effective leaders is their passion for their work and to some extent for the people who help them accomplish their work. The passion goes beyond enthusiasm and often expresses itself as an obsession for achieving company goals. The obsession for achieving company goals directly relates to seeing the big picture. Company goals can also be framed as the purpose of the organization. A key goal of the building-supply company just mentioned might be to increase revenue by eight percent next year. But the purpose of the organization might be to help create housing, schools, and medical facilities for the region. Passion for the task therefore leads toward seeing the big-picture.

One of the ways in which an entrepreneur can inject passion into employees is to tell a "creation-of-the-enterprise" story. The story should inspire people by understanding how the entrepreneur's product or cause will make the world a better place. Howard Schultz, the founder and chairman of Starbucks provides an example. Schultz's story begins in 1961 when his father broke his ankle at work and was left without income, insurance, or any way to support his family. The family's fear inspired change. Schultz grew up driven to create a company in which employees have a safety net woven of respect and dignity.[71] You will observe that the big-picture for Schultz here was a company providing a safety net for employees.

A major contributor to being passionate about work is to have a strong work ethic. If you believe that all honest work serves an important purpose, you are more likely to be passionate about your daily tasks. Assume that Sarah is a petroleum engineer working at an oil-processing plant. She believes in working hard every day, and also believes that the world still runs on petroleum despite the controversy about fossil fuels. Sarah is passionate about petroleum engineering also because she believes that what she does helps heats homes and workplaces and makes the cost of private transportation feasible.

Longer-Term Time Perspective

A fundamental characteristic of big-picture thinkers is that they have a longer-term time perspective than people who focus on the little-picture. Imagine that a family of four is on a 600-mile long automobile trip to reach a vacation destination. Approximately three-hundred miles from home, the engine fails. After being hauled to the nearest service center, the repair manager delivers the wretched news. The vehicle needs a new or rebuilt motor, and it will take three days to purchase and install. The price for the labor and repairs will be around $4,000. Add to this cost the motel expenses of two nights and two rooms, plus all the meals

The little-picture perspective is certainly justified, with comments from family members, including these: "Our vacation is ruined. Who wanted to spend two nights in a small-town motel?" "We are adding $5,000 to the cost of this vacation, with no extra fun in return." "These are the worst three days of my life." But Brian, the father in the family, introduces a longer-term time perspective to the situation: "I know this is bad, but in one year from now we will all laugh at the situation. Besides that, our car will last longer because we will have a new motor. And maybe will have a little fun exploring this strange town on foot."

Workers within an organization who have a long-range time perspective are also better able to see the big picture. The reverse is also true: Employees who tend to look at the big-picture are likely to have a longer-range time perspective. During a significant downturn in sales, accompanied by cost cutting layoffs, many employees become discouraged, and find it difficult to invest their full energy into the job. Yet those employees with a big-picture perspective are often able to look at the long-term and think, "We are in the bad part of the business cycle right now. In another year, the company will be booming once again, and we will be asked to help recruit friends and relatives to work here once again."

Farsightedness and Conceptual Thinking

A comprehensive characteristic of big-picture thinkers is farsightedness, the ability to understand the long-range implications of actions. The same characteristic is needed to develop visions and organizational strategy. The long-range consequences of actions are a vital component of seeing the big-picture.

A farsighted leader recognizes that hiring talented workers today will give the firm a long-range competitive advantage.

And a farsighted homeowner will recognize that investing in planting saplings outside the house now, will result in a beautiful lawn ten years from now (assuming that most of the trees survive). A more shortsighted view for the leader would be to hire less talented workers to satisfy immediate employment needs. The farsighted leader or manager is not oblivious to short-range needs but will devise an intermediate solution, such as hiring temporary workers until people with the right talents are found.

Conceptual thinking refers to the ability to see the overall perspective, and it makes it possible to be farsighted. We reinforce again the idea that a conceptual thinker is also a systems thinker because he or she understands how different parts of the organization influence each other. The human resources specialist who is successful in hiring high-caliber customer support workers will eventually influence company revenue. Assume that customers call in, or use chat, get their problems by a knowledgeable and friendly customer support worker. These customers are more likely to remain as customers and purchase more goods and services from the company.

A conceptual thinker also recognizes how his or her organizational unit meshes with the outside world. The CEO of the discount merchandise chain we mentioned above has a firm grasp on how the firm fits into the external world. She explains that during the Great Recession many affluent women (and also many men) gave the firm a try. Yet eight years after the Great Recession ended, they are still shopping regularly at the chain. The CEO says, "In good times and bad, upscale shoppers like to think they are getting quality goods at a low price." One study showed that 28 percent of women who earn over $100,000 per year visit the stores in question at least several times per year.

Proactive Personality

Many people who are big-picture thinkers act on their own without waiting for directions, orders, or suggestions from others. Being proactive also means that they seize the initiative to look at the big picture. A person with a proactive personality is an active agent in taking control of forces around him or her and is therefore is more likely to be sensitive to opportunities. The accompanying self-quiz provides you and opportunity to think through your tendencies toward being a proactive personality.

Being proactive also helps the individual spot problems that need fixing and understand how the problem fits into the big-picture. A production technician in an automobile plant might spot that if the carpeting cover on the driver's side is not put back correctly, it could rest on the accelerator causing unanticipated acceleration. She tells her boss that this problem could cause accidents and result in a product recall (the big-picture).

A person with a proactive personality takes the initiative to bring about meaningful change because he or she sees that such change is needed. A CEO might notice that notice that employees are not sufficiently engaged in their work, and then make suggestions for improving engagement. He might then work with managers in the organization to implement activities likely to improvement employee engagement. Among them would be improving health-insurance benefits, giving more exciting job assignments, providing more career advice to employees. Managers could also explain more carefully how individual positions fit into the purpose of the organization. (The big picture wins again!)

Tendencies toward Being a Proactive Personality

Indicate on a 1-to-5 scale the extent of your agreement with the statements below: agree strongly (AS), agree (A), neutral (N), disagree (D), disagree strongly (DS).

Number	Statement	AS	A	N	D	DS
1.	I plan carefully for things that might go wrong.	5	4	3	2	1
2.	I don't worry about problems until after they have taken place.	5	4	3	2	1
3.	If I see something that is broken, I fix it.	5	4	3	2	1
4.	I have been told several times that I am good at taking the initiative.	5	4	3	2	1
5.	I often let things like a computer password expire without making the necessary changes.	5	4	3	2	1
6.	When something important needs doing, I wait for somebody else to take the initiative.	5	4	3	2	1
7.	I think that having a home	5	4	3	2	1

	security system is a good investment of money.					
8.	I look around for good opportunities that would help me in my career or personal life.	5	4	3	2	1
9.	I don't give much thought to the future because there is not much I can do about it.	5	4	3	2	1
10.	It is a good idea to start saving or investing for retirement at the beginning of your career.	5	4	3	2	1

Scoring and Interpretation:

Total the numbers corresponding to your answers, and make these probable interpretations:

40–50 You have strong tendencies toward being a proactive personality. Such proactivity should be (or already is) an asset to you in your career and personal life.

28–39 You have about average tendencies toward being proactive. To enhance your success and have more fun in life, you might attempt to become more proactive.

10–27 You have a problem with proactivity. Both your work and personal life would probably be enhanced if you became more proactive.

Source: The idea for this scale and several of its statements stem from Thomas S. Bateman and J. Michael Crant: *The Proactive Component of Organizational Behavior: A Measure and Correlates*, Journal of Organizational Behavior, March 1993, p. 112.

A Few Suggestions for Action

1. To be an effective big-picture thinker, it is helpful to supplement focusing on ideas with focusing on facts. A balance between ideas and facts makes for more effective problem solving and decision making.
2. An effective approach to enhancing your skills as a big-picture thinker is to be more open to experience in the sense of developing your intellectual curiosity. For example, you might observe a street vendor selling artisan jewelry. If your purchase an item for the artisan ask him or her about how the jewelry is produced, and how he or she finds ideas for the designs.
3. A practical way of getting ideas for becoming a big-picture thinker is to gather insights from many people, including customers, employees, coworkers, and company leaders. Displaying a genuine interest in listening to these people will facilitate gathering the insights.
4. Making an effort to think divergently in terms of searching for more alternative solutions when solving a problem will enhance big-picture thinking. One of the alternatives you find might suggest a broad purpose of your work activity.
5. Intuition and big-picture thinking go hand in hand, so it is useful to pay careful attention to your quick emotional reaction to a problem facing you. The intuitive response will often relate to the broad purpose of what you are doing.

6. Being passionate about the task will often lead to big-picture thinking, so it is helpful to concentrate some effort into those aspects of your work that you find to be the most interesting.
7. Developing a long-range perspective is part of big-picture thinking. When you are facing a frustrating situation it is particularly helpful to visualize a long-range, positive outcome to the vexing situation you face.
8. Focusing on being proactive will often increase the probability that the big picture will come into view. The reason is that the proactive person will see opportunities or problems with big implications for the organization.

Chapter 5

Big-Picture Thinking and the Delay of Gratification

A problem facing many people is a tendency to seek immediate gratification of some need or want rather than going for longer term gratification and a bigger reward. In contrast, those people who focus on the big picture, or long-term rewards, wind up with more sustainable satisfaction. Delayed gratification is the ability to resist the temptation of an immediate reward and wait for a bigger reward that will occur because of the delay.

Visualize Kristol, an industrial engineer, whose hopes for the future include becoming an operations-executive. Kristol thinks with good reason that her chances of achieving her career goal would increase if she obtained an MBA degree. Kristol makes some inquiries and finds out that she can obtain an MBA in two years of part-time study at a local university. Kristol now faces a conflict between short-term and long-term gratification. If she adds an MBA program to her already busy schedule, she will surrender a lot of time she could spend in social and leisure activities as well as starting a family. Yet Kristol's big picture of becoming an operations-executive in the future propels her to give up these many important short-term gratifications in order to achieve a big payoff in the future. Kristol is taking a risk because there are no guarantees that (a) she will successfully complete her degree or that (b) the MBA will facilitate her becoming an operations executive. Yet prudent risk taking is characteristic of big-picture thinkers because the little picture usually already exists and is more of a sure thing.

The accompanying checklist will be helpful in examining your own tendencies toward searching for instant gratification versus delaying gratification.

The Instant Gratification Checklist

To help you think through your tendencies toward searching for instant gratification, go through the following checklist:

Statement of How Instant Gratification Influences My Thinking or Behavior

Statement Relating to Instant Gratification	*(X)*
1. Why should a person work to get a college degree when he or she can get a job right now?	
2. During a job search I would take the first plausible offer I received.	

3.	A six-year car loan is a good way to manage finances if a person decides to purchase an expensive car.
4.	Have fun today and let the future take care of itself.
5.	It's a good idea to buy oneself a treat rather than spend money on preventive maintenance on a vehicle or a home heating and cooling unit.
6.	A person taking up tennis or golf should jump right in and have fun rather than going through the work of taking lessons.
7.	Saving and investing for retirement is usually a bad idea because it deprives you of a lot of fun you could have in the present.
8.	I approve of people checking their Facebook or Twitter accounts every half hour rather than staying focused on their work.
9.	It's a good idea to get an advance on a tax refund by paying a fee to the tax preparer.
10.	If I were in a supermarket with a three-year old, and the child was crying and screaming because he or she wanted a candy bar, I would buy the child the candy just shut him or her up.
11.	It is acceptable for a person to get drunk at a party occasionally because you only live once.
12.	Going through this checklist is boring. I would rather go do something else.
13.	Living for the moment is better than worrying about the future.

14. Even if I lived in a very cold climate, I would prefer to purchase expensive tickets for an entertainment event than purchase snow tires.	
15. If I were the hiring manager, I would make a job offer to the first reasonable candidate rather than searching for an ideal one.	

Scoring and Interpretation: The higher the number of statements you checked as fitting your thinking or behavior, the stronger your tendency toward looking for instant gratification rather than waiting for a bigger reward later on. Too much focus on instant- or short-term gratification could mean that you are not paying serious enough attention to the big picture. The fewer the number of statements that you checked, the stronger your tendency toward delaying gratification and thereby aiding you to keep the big picture in mind.

The Famous Marshmallow Experiment with Preschool Children

Many readers have probably read about the marshmallow experiment that popularized the importance of delaying gratification. Yet a preliminary experiment with cookies preceded the more famous experiment. In 1970, psychologist Walter Mischel decided to place a cookie in front of a group of children and give them a choice. The children could either eat the cookie on the spot, or they could wait until Mischel returned from a brief errand, and then be rewarded with a second cookie. The children who did not wait would be allowed to eat only the first cookie. Consistent with the mentality of most young children, once Michel left the room, many children ate the cookie right away. Yet, a few children delayed eating the first cookie long enough to receive the second. These patient youngsters were labeled high-delay children, giving Mischel the idea to further explore this phenomenon of delayed gratification.

In the follow-up experiment, Mischel and his colleagues offered a group of four-year old children the choice of one marshmallow immediately or two marshmallows if they could wait 15 minutes. The children were brought one at a time into a room, shown the marshmallow, and offered a deal. They could eat the marshmallow right now or if the waited until the experimenter returned (about a fifteen-minute interval), they would get a second marshmallow to eat long with the first one. The children who waited found ways to distract themselves until the experimenter returned.

The experimenters later found out something else, thanks to a happy coincidence. Mischel's daughters were attending the same school, located on the Stanford University campus, where the marshmallow experiments were conducted. Mischel kept hearing from his daughters that the classmates who failed to wait for the second marshmallow got into more trouble than the others, both in school and out of school.

The researchers later tracked down hundreds of students who had participated in the experiments, and assessed the outcomes achieved by these children as they became adults. The researchers found that the children who resisted temptation (labelled "high delayers") achieved greater academic success, better health, and lower rates of marital separation and divorce. The researchers concluded that the ability to delay gratification provided a protective buffer against the development of being vulnerable in many situations in later life.

In a third study, 1,000 children were studied from birth until age 32. A major finding of the study was that strong self-control in childhood was related to future physical health, less substance dependence, better personal finances, and fewer criminal offenses. The same findings occur occurred even when other factors such as intelligence and social class were relatively equal. Equally illuminating, when sibling pairs were compared, the sibling in each pair with lower self-control had poorer life outcomes, despite being raised in the same household.[72]

Another aspect of Mischel's studies reinforces the importance of rational thinking for the delay of gratification. By varying the situation the experimenters gained insight into what enables children to wait in order to achieve a bigger reward. Waiting for a reward was found to be more difficult for the children in the experiment when they focused on the hot, or emotional aspect of the reward. Waiting was found to be easier when focused on the cool, or intellectual aspect. The intellectual aspect of the reward was framed in terms of thinking of the marshmallow as little fluffy clouds, whereas the emotional aspect was thinking of the sweetness and chewy texture of the marshmallow.[73]

An interpretation of these findings is that is that if you focus on the cognitive aspect of a reward, you will be able to delay gratification longer than if you focus on the emotional aspect. Imagine that while browsing a new-car dealership Ben sees a new SUV that excites him. He conjures up the feeling of the scent of the new vehicle, and how proud he will be driving the $45,000 beauty. These emotional features prod him toward making the purchase right now. In contrast, if Ben focuses on the cognitive aspects of the situation, such as still owing money on his present vehicle, he is more likely to wait another year before making the purchase.

So what do these experiments about delaying gratification, and the observation of delayers being more successful in later life, have to do with big-picture thinking? The point is that delaying gratification now enables a person to achieve the big picture of receiving a more substantial reward later. And if Ben waits another year or two to purchase a SUV when he has paid for his present vehicle, he achieves the big picture of less financial pressure.

To Delay Gratification, First Define Your Big Picture

As mentioned in the outset of the chapter, in Kristol's situation, having a big picture in mind directs us toward delaying gratification in order to achieve a worthwhile future end. At its best, the big picture is a grand purpose in life. Ben Carson is the director of HUD (Housing and Urban Development) under the Trump administration, and former director of pediatric neurosurgery at the Johns Hopkins Children's Center. Dr. Carson is the originator of groundbreaking surgical procedures, the most famous being the separation of South African Siamese twins joined at the head.

Carson says that his professional accomplishments, including a philanthropic foundation, have been guided by the big picture, defined as a vision worth living for. (Carson's vision included helping children overcome neurological problems, and later grew to guiding people in poverty to uplift themselves.) He believes that this vision calls for the best of his talents, energy, and focus.

In reflecting on his childhood, Carson says that poverty helped he and his brother, Curtis, learn the importance of the life-impacting principle of delayed gratification. Living in poverty, the boys and their mother had to wait a long time for a reward such as a car for the family or a used bike. The mother assured the boys that they would not always be poor, but that the family's financial progress would require time and effort. The same principle of delayed gratification was applied to acquiring knowledge of academic subjects. The mother instructed the Carson boys that they could find eventual career success if they followed the road of education to its natural end.

Carson writes that the desire for instant gratification and short-term gratification is responsible for the problems many high-school students face in preparation for adulthood. A good example is that being "cool" in school translates into showing little respect for teachers and in contrast, the nerdier students respect the authority of teachers and recognize the value of acquiring formal knowledge. To the less cool students, the big picture is being an informed, responsible person with a rewarding career. In the short range, the cooler students are more popular, yet in many cases the less-cool students have a better future.[74]

This analysis does not imply that later in life a person cannot be cool and have a good career. We simply mean that when a desire to be cool in the present and the near-future blocks long-range, big-picture thinking the delayed gratification of a prosperous career might not be forthcoming.

For some people a clearly defined big picture surfaces in early life so they do not have to give it much thought. Zach might be so enamored with taking care of pets early in life that he develops a big picture of someday operating a veterinary clinic so he can care to the health needs of hundreds of domestic animals. He could therefore bring happiness to pets and their owners. Ivy might grow up in a large family that operates a few automobile dealerships. She perceives operating a dealership to be a preferred lifestyle, and therefore develops the big picture of being the successful manager of one of the dealerships. Other people have to invest mental effort in developing a big picture, much like developing a mission in life.

Recommended steps for identifying your big picture, or mission, include answering the following questions:

- What are my five biggest wishes or hopes?
- What do I want to accomplish in my career during the next five years? (You might extent this this time period, but an intermediate-term goal of five years might seem more attainable.)
- What do I want to accomplish in my personal life during the next five years?
- Who am I?
- What do I want to accomplish in life?

Adrienne R. Lofton, the senior vice president, global brand manager at Under Armour, used a mission statement to help power her career and give her a big picture of what she wanted to accomplish. She regarded every job she had ever taken as getting closer to becoming a CMO. She said earlier in her career, "From the beginning of my career I would write five-year plans for myself and talk about them with my key mentors, identifying areas I needed to strengthen to get where I wanted to be."[75]

Another approach that contributes to formulating a mission and understanding the big picture you are pursuing is to focus on the values supporting what you are attempting to accomplish. Russ Harris observes, "When we face major challenges in life, if we move forward guided by our values, we will feel a sense of meaning and purpose. And we will find satisfaction in knowing what we are doing really matters to us."[76] Assume that Gordon holds the value that helping people accomplish financial security contributes substantially to society. Part of his big picture is becoming a certified financial planner (CFP) so he can obtain the formal credentials to help people plan their financial future. Gordon will forego many instances of immediate gratification, such as watching football on television, so he can study for the CFP exam.

Delaying Gratification by Focusing on Your Intermediate-Term or Long-Term Goal

As implied by using a mission statement to establish your big picture, you will also need to frequently delay gratification to attain an intermediate-term or long-term goal. Brain chemistry can sometimes work against the person who wants to delay gratification in order to attain a longer-range goal. Quite often an instant fix releases dopamine, a hormone associated with pleasure. Dopamine can be released in many ways including eating something sweet, gambling, and watching pornography. Conrad, a husband and father, might have the four-year goal of saving enough money for a down payment on a house for the family. Today, however, he feels the need for instant gratification so goes online to place some bets on sporting events. Unfortunately he blows $2,000 on losing bets. Accumulating enough money for the down payment on the house is delayed further into the future.

In defense of people who seek instant gratification, metabolism can sometimes prod us toward impulsivity. Biochemist Bill Gordon explains that studies have shown that increasing blood glucose levels led to an increase in the value placed on future rewards. (In other words, with more sugar in the blood you have less craving for a quick fix.) Conversely, drinking a beverage without sugar leads to an increase in the value placed on immediate rewards. With less blood sugar a person is likely to be more impulsive, and put aside a longer term perspective, as well as the big picture.[77] The preceding information might be helpful in explain some types of impulsive behavior. Nevertheless, be cautious in thinking that if you eat candy or ice cream, or drink beverages with sugar that you will become immediately effective in delaying gratification as a way of attaining longer-range goals.

The problem of procrastination provides another illustration of how delay of gratification is linked to focusing on intermediate-term or long- term goals. A major reason for procrastination is that a person wants to gratify an immediate need instead of sticking with a task that requires time to complete.[78] The person wants to feel good at the moment rather than reap future rewards. The person might think, "Why work on my portion of the cost reduction report right now. I'll go across the street and get a latté, and then feel more like tacking the cost-reduction report."

Another example of an impulsive report that triggers procrastination is "I'll get my résumé update for HR a little later. Right now it would be much more fun to send my Facebook friends a great joke I read about a horse going into a bar." The person who procrastinates to seek immediate gratification must focus on gradually controlling his or her impulsiveness and think more about longer-term rewards.

An additional insight into delaying gratification in order to attain longer-term goals is that you need to engage the part of the brain responsible for planning, the frontal lobe. The frontal lobe is located in the frontal and upper area of the cortex, and carries out high mental processes such as thinking, decision making, and planning. Parts of the inner brain, amygdala and the hippocampus, are more involved with emotion.

It would be far-fetched to think that a person can send a direct command to the frontal lobe in the same manner that he or she can consciously move the right or left leg. What a person can do is think, "This is the time to be rational instead of being so emotional." A company vice president might think that a new office assistant is an outstanding beauty. The vice president's hormones begin to range, and he thinks, "How much fun it would be to hit on this lovely young lady." Upon reflection, he then thinks, "I'm letting my emotions take over. It's time to exercise logic and recognize that if I hit on her it could wind up tarnishing my reputation."

Delay of Gratification as Part of Self-Discipline and Willpower

The self-disciplined person can readily delay gratification because the delay of gratification is a key component of self-discipline. In the context used here, self-discipline is the ability to work systematically and progressively toward a goal until it is achieved. If you have a high degree of self-discipline, you work toward your goals without being derailed by the many distractions faced each day, and perhaps each hour.

Self-disciplined people are willing to put aside immediate pleasure to achieve a goal that goes beyond the present moment. Quite often delay of gratification entails trading a lesser reward now for a bigger reward later. For example, a disciplined industrial sales representative will forgo a couple of quick sales now in order to cultivate a customer with the potential for a much bigger sale. (Yes, despite the overwhelming amount of business-to-business sales on the Internet, most large companies still have sales representatives calling on customers.)

The decision to delay gratification is often difficult. During a job search the less-disciplined person will accept the first job offer that comes along, even if it pays less than what he or she needs and does not contribute to career growth. In urgent need of money and feeling anxious and insecure about being unemployed, the person's actions are understandable. Yet looking at the long range, as well as the big picture, taking a job that does not pay enough to meet expenses could well mean that a new job search will have to begin soon.

Delay of gratification also refers to minimizing shortcuts in order to attain long-term success. The shortcut may be a quick fix—and therefore gratifying—but will result in lesser long-term rewards. An example is that a building owner might need a costly roof replacement. Instead he opts for a repair that costs one-fifth as much which is gratifying for now. Unfortunately for him, other parts of the roof soon need repair, and it becomes obvious that it would have been better to use self-discipline to find a way to finance a new roof when the problem first surfaced.

Closely related to self-discipline and willpower, the delay of gratification can be considered an expression of ego control. As described by psychologists Jack Block and David Funder, ego control is a person's general tendency to inhibit impulses.[79] On the low end of the continuum are under-controlled individuals who act out their desires without concern for the future. (A low ego-control person might think, "Why not drink six beers tonight, I don't have to worry about going to work until Monday.") At the other end of the continuum are over-controlled individuals who restrain themselves even when not necessary. (A person with excessive ego control might think, "I would like to have a caramel sundae for dessert but if I do, I could get started on a path to sugar addiction.")

Both too little and too much ego control can work against a person's well-being in terms of attaining long-term goals. The person with weak ego control behaves impulsively and may neglect the big picture of a brighter future. A representative example would be the person described above who used money earmarked for a house down payment to gamble online.

The problem with too strong ego control in terms of the future is that the individual may avoid risk taking, thereby missing out on potential big rewards. Assume that Janis, a middle manager, has lost her job as part of a company downsizing. After conducting a job search for several months, she concludes that he most likely will not be able to replace her former position. Next, Janice explores the possibility of finding another career. She hits upon the idea of purchasing a franchise as a way of running a business and earning a decent income. After researching various possibilities, she decides that investing in a vehicle glass replacement business would be a good idea. The franchise would cost $35,000 to get started, and Janice has more than sufficient money saved to make that payment. Having too much ego control, Janice pulls back. She fears taking the risk of investing in the franchise even though industry data suggest that it is a prudent risk. For now, Janice has bypassed an opportunity to live out her big picture of owning and operating a successful small business.

Willpower, Grit, and the Big Picture

Closely related to the idea of using ego control to delay gratification is the better known concept of willpower. The latter is an old-fashioned idea that has surged in popular use and scientific investigation in recent years. The term willpower generally refers to the ability or power to practice self-control. Through willpower, people are able to delay short-term gratification in order to achieve a more important intermediate-term or long-term goal that is an integral part of a person's big picture.

As with identifying your big picture, willpower begins with establishing a mission and goal. It is much easier to exercise self-control when you have a well-defined purpose in life, along with goals to support that purpose. With a mission and goal, you are better able to delay gratification because your personal big picture stays in the back of your mind. Margot, a chief marketing officer with strong willpower, might reflect, "I will resist using my expense account to partially fund a family vacation because I want to maintain a reputation for high ethics."

Part of Margot's willpower stems for her mission in life. She wants to be a well-respected affluent member of her community who makes an impact on the world. At the same time, Margot has a couple of intermediate goals that reinforce her mission: She wants to receive a performance bonus this year, and she wants to help establish a culture of high ethics in her company. Being discovered and publicly reported for misusing corporate resources by partially funding family vacation expenses with company money could readily damage accomplishing her mission and attaining her goals. As a result Margot may not realize her big picture.

Self-control is such a major component of willpower that the latter is usually defined as the ability to exercise self-discipline, as we mentioned. In understanding the importance of willpower and self- control for work and personal life, keep in mind that the two are used for many purposes in additional to regulating or preventing behavior. People spend a lot time resisting temptations that are important in attaining their big picture. Resisting the temptations of high caloric and high-cholesterol food, and excessive consumption of alcoholic beverages supports the big picture of living a long and healthy life.

Another useful way of understanding the relationship between willpower and self-control, is that willpower is the engine of self-control. Management trainer Joe Robinson writes that this engine powers the ability to manage thoughts, emotions, and harmful habits, and override them for long-range benefits. As a result gratification is delayed in the service of attaining the big picture. Robinson explains that entrepreneurs need this type of self-control to deal with the difficulties that swarm like hornets when one embarks on a self-made path.[80] For example, an entrepreneur might develop a system for freeze-drying food that will last twenty-five years to be stored at home. However, sophisticated and effective this technology might be, the entrepreneur faces the enormous challenge of finding customers.

A highly useful approach to willpower is to put it under the umbrella of grit. As defined by psychology professor, Angela Duckworth and her colleagues who have researched this human quality, grit is perseverance and passion for long-term goals.[81] Grit therefore helps us see our way through to attaining the big picture. The gritty person is willing to devote may years to attaining an important goal, such as becoming a professional athlete, successful inventor, or a CEO.

The person with grit often wins out over more talented people, because grit gives you the stamina for the long haul. As frequently observed by industrial sales managers, the sales representatives who earn the most commissions are not necessarily those with the best persuasive skills and personal appearance. Instead, the winningest reps are those who have decent natural sales skills and who keep plugging along with logical proposals for the long haul.

I am reminded of a sales rep for one of the highest price heavy duty trucks on the market that sell for about $500,000. In a social setting, I asked the rep how long it took to sell such an expensive truck. He replied, "On the average close to two years." Despite the two-year closing cycle, the rep was making a good living. It takes a lot of grit to wait two years to earn a commission. You might say this rep was selling long-haulers for the long-haul of attaining is big picture of being a success in his field.

Another key use of willpower is for the purpose of resisting temptation. Willpower is obviously needed to resist temptation in order to delay gratification of a short-term goal to attain a more important long-term goal. Imagine that business planner Anthony has to submit a plan to the CEO by Monday on how the company can capture a share of the market for home appliances in Brazil. Anthony estimates he needs about five more hours of concentrated work to compete his plan. Today is Sunday, and Anthony has already agreed to participate in family activities for the morning. Dinner, getting the children ready for bed, and catching up with the news will take up much of the evening. The one chunk of discretionary time for Anthony is the afternoon.

Anthony's ability to exercise willpower to resist temptation will be challenged because there is a telecast of his favorite NFL team this afternoon. Having strong willpower, Anthony will resist the temptation of watching football in order to invest the entire afternoon to working on the business plan. (Perhaps he will take a five-minute break every thirty minutes to check on the score.) At the same time, he will resist the subtle temptation of falling prey to the common sentiment, "Who works on Sunday afternoon?"

Delay of Gratification for the Big Picture of Financial Success

Personal finance is an aspect of life in which the delay of gratification has an enormous payoff in terms of achieving a long-term that facilitates attaining a positive big picture. Mastering delayed gratification has been acknowledged as the key to financial success. Purchasing goods and services now that are not essential or bring small satisfaction, often blocks the future purchase of goods and services that offer major rewards. A common example is a person paying so much for smartphone service that he or she cannot put aside enough money to purchase a reliable vehicle needed to go back and forth from a job.

Consumer debt can be considered the process of using dollars earned in the future to pay for current expenses, with future payments that include interest charges and perhaps fees.

At times debt is a necessity, such as not having enough money to pay for home repairs, large medical expenses, or the purchase of a home or vehicle. So these types of expenses might be considered outside the realm of instant gratification. Data about credit card debt are illuminating. In 2016, average American household debt was $5,700 not including a home mortgage. The average debt for a balance-carrying household was $16,048. The average annual interest on credit-card debt was $1,292.[82]

With large amounts of debt in relation to household income, many people almost forced to increase their amount of indebtedness. The problem is that because the person has such large debt payments, it becomes extremely difficult to pay cash for goods and services, or to pay off credit card debt at the end of the month.

Here are two financial examples of the difference between immediate gratification and delayed gratification that can block a person from experiencing the big picture of a better life.

- A couple spends a big chunk of their income to rent a luxurious apartment. As a result the couple cannot save enough money to purchase a house they would really like to own. If instead, they delayed gratification by renting a modest apartment for now, the two could set aside money to save toward a down payment on a house.

- A man who dislikes his job as a delivery driver decides that he needs a mood elevator, so he searches for immediate gratification by spending $2,500 on a cruise vacation. Assume instead, he delays gratification by investing that money in a community college program to qualify for another field, such as an ambulance medic or a heating and air conditioning technician. In this way he might have experienced the big picture of a satisfying career.

Finance blogger Lance Cothern offers a few suggestions to reduce the immediate gratification of impulse buying, thereby enabling you to attain delayed gratification. Write down your financial goals and hold yourself accountable. Before purchasing merchandise or a service consider if this is something you need or want. If the purchase is something you merely want, wait twenty-four hours before going through with the purchase. Also, ask a wise and experienced person about their biggest money regrets, and see if there is a lesson in the regret for you.[83]

Techniques for Delaying Gratification in Service of Your Big Picture

Even with a slight or moderate disposition toward impulsivity, it is possible to use everyday techniques to delay gratification. People at the upper end of impulsivity may first require counseling with a mental health professional before they can capitalize on the techniques described next to delay gratification.[84]

1. A key first step in delaying gratification is to reflect on whether you really want the bigger rewards stemming from intermediate- term, or long-term gratification. A non-delayer might think, "I don't care about needing a new hot water heater for the house, I am going online to pay $2,500 for a Super Bowl ticket right now. My purpose in life is to have fun." A delayer facing the same circumstance might say, "It would be fun

watching the Super Bowl in person but having a reliable stream of hot water is more important for my peace of mind."

2. Closely related to the first step is to know your values and goals. When you know what is important to you, it is easier to identify courses of action that lead to happiness and success. Visualize Luis who strongly values an independent lifestyle which to him would include owning and operating a small business. To accomplish this feat, he will most likely have to borrow money to supplement whatever funds he acquires on his own. Borrowing money at sensible interest rates requires a good credit record. As a result, Luis will avoid getting far in debt by purchasing with a credit card, loads of unessential merchandise and services.

Another example of values influencing instant versus delayed gratification would be the value a person places on being debt free versus the value of an expensive possession. The person who wants to be debt free might choose to purchase an attractive watch for $50, whereas the person who values luxury might borrow $8,000 to purchase a German watch advertised in *The Wall Street Journal*.

Values lead naturally to goals because we pursue what is important to us. In the case of Luis, he values independence and therefore established the goal of becoming a small-business operator. Another example of a goal that would make it easier to delay gratification would be aspiring toward a promotion. Tanya is a CPA in a large accounting firm, and she aspires to being placed on a track toward becoming a partner in her firm. One of Tanya's favorite leisure activities is to patronize night clubs with a few close friends. While at a club for a couple of hours it would be easy for Tanya to drink enough alcoholic beverages to surpass the blood alcohol level for safe driving. With the goal in mind of becoming a partner in her firm, Tanya resists the instant gratification of having three drinks because she knows she would be at risk for getting caught driving under the influence of alcohol.

3. The combination of values and goals leads naturally to creating a plan for delaying gratification. The plan specifies what steps need to be taken to delay gratification enough to attain the long-term goal that fulfills one or more important values. In the case of Luis, his plan might include incurring a moderate amount of debt in order to establish a good credit rating. The reason for the moderate amount of debt might be counterintuitive. If a person never borrows money, however, he or she has no history of success in repaying loans.

4. Establish priorities for the importance of what you want to achieve in life. The general purpose of prioritizing is to pinpoint which activities and goals require the most delay of gratification. One of Clarissa's goals might be to attain a body-mass index of 18 (considered to be a very healthy number, taking into account height and weight). Yet her goal of becoming a nurse practitioner is much more important. Clarissa might therefore allow herself the occasional indulgence of binge eating. Yet she would not opt for the instant gratification of watching television instead of studying for an exam in pharmacology.

5. Give yourself an occasional reward for delaying gratification. A sensible approach to frequent delay of

gratification to attain a long-term goal and the big picture is to self-reward along the way for good progress. It might seem paradoxical, but a reasonable amount of instant gratification can be a reward for delay of gratification. The reward technique works best if you have divided your long-term goal into short-term goals.

Back to Clarissa, the aspiring nurse practitioner. She is currently working as a registered nurse but wants to upgrade her credentials and knowledge to become a nurse practitioner. She is working on a master's degree part time, including weekends. All the difficult attending class and studying demands considerable focus. Her sub-goals include passing one course at a time and attaining a good grade. As she completes each course she might "go crazy" for a couple of days and indulge herself in any way she wants, and not think about studying.

A Few Suggestions for Action

1. A major insight to be gathered from the relationship between delay of gratification and the big picture is that the delay will in many situations have a big payoff. The happiness and success forthcoming from attaining a well thought through big picture is usually worth the small sacrifices of delaying short-term gratification.
2. You will typically need to exercise considerable self-discipline to delay gratification in order to attain intermediate-term and long-term goals. Self-discipline plays a major role because you have to stay focused on a longer-range goal of delayed satisfaction. A recurring example is that people performing analytical work such as preparing a report or budget, have to minimize giving into the temptation of regularly checking e-mail and social media sites unrelated to the task at hand.

Chapter 6

Special Skills and Actions of Big-Picture Thinkers

Throughout this book we have been describing directly and indirectly the actions and thinking of big-picture thinkers. In this chapter we take a closer look at how big-picture thinkers go about key facets of their work and personal life. Equally important, the ideas in this chapter might reinforce what you are already doing to be a big-picture thinker.

To illustrate what we mean by the skills and actions of big-picture thinkers, one section of this chapter describes how big-picture thinkers are good team players because they are concerned about the good of the team and the organization. Such information would reinforce a person's recognition of the importance of thinking big about team play. In the words of Andrew Carnegie, "Teamwork is the ability to work together toward a common vision. It is the ability to direct individual accomplishments toward organizational objectives. It is also the fuel that allows common people to attain uncommon results."

Studying the skills and actions (behaviors) of big-picture thinkers will give you some new ideas for becoming a big-picture thinker and doer. As you dig into the skills and actions of big-picture thinkers, keep in mind a subtle but significant point—the arrow runs in both directions.

For example, the observation is presented later in this chapter that during negotiation, big-picture thinkers begin with a plausible demand and offer. The plausible demand or offer facilitates achieving a successful outcome to the negotiation. If you keep in mind that you should begin negotiation with a plausible demand or offer, such actions will help you develop into a big-picture thinker. The same two-directional arrow applies to other skills and actions of big-picture thinkers. If you consistently practice the skills and actions of big-picture thinkers, you will enhance your ability to be such a thinker.

Minimizing Minutiae

By definition, a key behavior of big-picture thinkers is their ability to avoid getting bogged down in minutiae. Career advisor Karen Burns believes that big-picture people are more effective at their work and enjoy it more because they do not get bogged down in the minutiae of their jobs. Getting bogged down in details can result in not understanding one's professional roles in the overall scheme of things.[85]

Assume that Shelby is an environmental engineer working for a large company. Her broad role is helping the company conserve environmental resources in including energy, water, physical products. She also wants to help the company control its use of toxins that might harm the environment. Yet sometimes Shelby fails to keep her big role in mind, and instead focuses on minutiae. She begins to obsess over whether anybody, anywhere in the company is failing to place plastic bottles or aluminum cans in recycling bins. Shelby constructs a detection scheme accompanied by an elaborate database about failures to properly recycle bottles and cans. Soon Shelby neglects the reality that she should be making broader recommendations to the company about the conservation of environmental resources.

To help overcome getting bogged down in minutiae, think about the purpose of your role in the organization as well as the purpose of your organization. For some types of work, understanding your role and the purpose of the organization is relatively easy, such as being in charge of franchise sales for Papa John's Pizza. In contrast, if you have a position such as industry analyst for a firm that sells research information about industry trends, it becomes more difficult to explain the purpose of what you and your company are doing.

One method of understanding the big picture of your role and that of your employer is to imagine how you would respond if in a social situation, a stranger asked you "What do you do?" If you can provide a one-minute explanation of your role and the purpose of your company, you have a good fix on the big picture. If the stranger walks away with a shrug, you might be focusing too much on the minutiae.

Breaking the Rules

A big-picture thinker will occasionally break the rules of conventional behavior because he or she is focused on an important goal and attaining that goal might require a different path to success. Tyler is thinking of a career in corporate law, and his big picture is to become a partner in a leading law firm. The unwritten rule for being recruited into a prestigious law firm is to graduate from one of the elite law schools. But unconventional thinking Tyler has a different idea. He has observed that top-level law firms have been accused of too much homogeneity in their recruiting. As a result, in recent years these law firms have looked toward recruiting from a broader base of law schools. Tyler proceeds with his off-the-beaten-track career path and studies law at a low- ranking law school in a small city far away from elite corporate law firms. To Tyler's delight, he is hired by a prestigious law firm, and he is on the first rung of the ladder of attaining his big picture of becoming a partner in the law firm.

Abe Issa, the founder of Global Efficient Energy, represents an extreme example of breaking the rules because he saw things as they could be, not as they were—his big picture. The first rule he broke was selling against the tide. Issa's company provides foam insulation, HVAC, LED lighting and solar energy products in Texas, the heart of oil and gas country. Another unwritten rule Issa broke was that he launched his company through door-to-door sales, much like the Fuller Brush Man and Avon Lady of yesteryear.

Friends, business associates and investors told Issa that he would have almost zero success in selling energy products to homeowners. These people explained to Issa that he had no track record, no references, no office, and no employees. Furthermore, he would be knocking on doors uninvited. But naysayers could not stop Issa from pursuing his vision. He knew that energy costs are a major expense for homeowners. Cutting these expenses would be a good value proposition even such methods ran counter to the use of traditional energy sources in Fort Worth, Texas.

Among the unfriendly responses he received as he went door-to-door attempting to sell his products and services were, "Not interested." "Don't need it." "Don't waste your time."

For every 100 sales calls, Issa might squeeze out about three appointments to do a free audit to demonstrate to homeowners the money they could save through more effective energy management. Issa persisted, and his firm thrives today, providing lower-cost energy to homes in Texas.[86] The young entrepreneur, born in Lebanon, has achieved his big picture in the United States.

Frequent Eureka Experiences

A key part of being creative is to have an "aha moment" also referred to as "Eureka!" After pondering a problem in the back of your mind, a flash of insight occurs about such matters as the need for a product or service, a brand name, or how to raise some quick cash. The same Eureka! Moment can occur in aspects outside the realm of creativity, including the need for a career change or how to improve a personal relationship. A blockbuster idea might break through in a flash of insight that is both unexpected and unusually clear.[87] The person might decide suddenly that it is time to exercise more financial discipline, search for a new job, or find a mate.

A Eureka! Moment can sometimes be triggered by suddenly questioning a ritual. Take Clyde who has been struggling to stop smoking for several years. He has been successful in reducing smoking but chaining it to limited activities, one by one. Clyde no longer smokes when walking the street, driving his car, during working hours, or with family members. Persistent Clyde now smokes only when he consumes an alcoholic beverage. You guessed it—Clyde will often decide to have a drink because he really wants a cigarette. One sunny late afternoon, on his way home from golf, Clyde has the urge for a cigarette. As a result he stops his car and enters the first convenience store he finds. He purchases a single can of beer, sits on a bus stop bench, and lights a cigarette. A Eureka! Moment flashes into Clyde's mind: "I'm a crazy cigarette addict. I just bought a beer to legitimize my smoking. I'm through with this craziness for good." Clyde throws away his half-full pack of cigarettes into a trash can, and never smokes again.

Big-picture thinkers have "aha! moments" more frequently because consciously and pre-consciously they are thinking about the meaning and consequences of events. A big-picture server or bus person might notice while clearing the tables that a certain meal, or portion of a meal, is frequently left half-eaten on plates. The server proceeds to tell the restaurant manager or owner, "It looks like our entrées would be more popular if we did not include asparagus for a vegetable."

David and Ellen Brennen had a Eureka! Moment that they think will pay big dividends for their business, Yellow Jacket and Fleet Feet Sports, a running shoes and apparel store in upstate New York. The couple noticed that retail sales associates had lost much of their former status. As observed by the Brennen couple, "You'd want to talk to that salesperson and get their information, and you'd want to know what's best for me and respect that. We believe that has fallen by the wayside."

To counteract this problem, the couple hit upon the idea of boosting their minimum wage to an astounding $20 an hour for approximately 50 employees by the end of 2021. This wage surpassed the $15 rate going into effect for New York City by 2021, and the $12. Fifty per hour for upstate New York at the end of 2020. By paying store associates so well, they will most likely feel professional, and act accordingly.

Taking a big-picture perspective, Ellen Brenner said they will create room for higher wages by paying off their business loans, a home mortgage and by finding operational efficiencies with suppliers and inventory management.[88]

An example of a "Eureka! Moment" from a large business enterprise took place at Nike Football. A designer team headed by Denis Dekovic noticed that in the existing design for football (soccer) shoes, they start below the ankle. Dekovic said "What we really wanted to design was a product that was not just for the foot but for the body." The new product stemming from this insight was the expensive Magista Obra, the first soccer shoe to rise above the ankle. The design echoes the network of ligaments connects the lower leg to the foot.[89] A link between this advanced soccer shoe (cleats) is that the design team had the big picture in mind that many factors can contribute to enhanced sports performance, including shoe design.

Being a Good Organizational Citizen

An employee attitude highly valued by employers is organizational citizenship behavior. The term refers to a willingness to go beyond one's job description to help coworkers or the company even if such an act does not lead to an immediate reward. By acting in this way, the person sees the big picture of the importance of coworkers performing well and the organization prospering. The person is willing to donate a little time and effort for the greater good.

Organizational citizenship behavior is so important to organizations that this set of attitudes has been the subject of many studies. A general finding has been that as a result of many workers being good organizational citizens, the organization functions more effectively in such ways as improved productivity, reduced costs, customer satisfaction, and reduced turnover. The good organizational citizen often has the big picture in mind of a smoother functioning, and more prosperous organization.

In addition to helping the company, employees who are good organizational citizens also benefit. They are likely to perform better, and as a result they obtain better performance reviews and salary increases.[90] By helping others, the highly perceptive worker will see a path to attaining the big picture of doing well himself or herself.

The accompanying self-assessment quiz gives you an opportunity to think through your actual or potential tendencies toward organizational citizenship behavior. Two examples of good organizational citizenship behavior follow:

- Kevin, a management trainee at a bank, observes that the office in which he works seems glum. So he goes out of his way to be cheerful to others and offers compliments for work well done. The big picture Kevin visualizes is a high-morale office.
- Chloe, a gifted information technician, is walking down the aisle toward her cubicle. She notices a coworker from another department with a panicked look on his face as he stares into his desktop computer screen. Chloe asks if she can help. She then proceeds to transfer valuable data from a corrupted document into a new document for the employee in panic. The big picture Chloe visualizes is an office in which worker are not panicked by ordinary technology problems.

My Tendencies toward Organizational Citizenship Behavior

Describe whether each of the statements in the quiz below is mostly true or mostly false about you. If you have not experienced the situation, estimate whether it would be most likely true or most likely false about you.

Number	Statement about Organizational Citizenship Behavior	Mostly True	Mostly False
1.	I have helped a coworker with a work problem without being asked.		
2.	I pick up litter in the company parking lot or outside of the building and then dispose of the litter properly.		
3.	Helping others is an important part of my job even if I am not a manager.		
4.	I make a special effort to say thank you and smile when somebody helps me in any way on the job.		
5.	I volunteer to do a non-glamorous task when nobody in particular has responsibility for the task.		
6.	If I found an apparently intoxicated person sleeping on the ground outside my workplace, I would call for help rather than leaving him or her lying there.		
7.	I am pretty good at putting myself in another worker's place and understanding his or her perspective.		
8.	I do my best to give effective comforting messages to other workers in distress.		

9.	I am able to initiate, maintain, and terminate casual conversations with coworkers.			
10.	During group meetings, I listen carefully to whoever is speaking to the group without performing another task, such as looking at a smartphone placed on my lap.			
11.	If my company faced an emergency such as a flood or hurricane, I would tell my supervisor that I will be on call twenty-four hours per day to help out.			
12.	I have covered for workers who were absent or out on a break.			
13.	I check with others before doing something that would affect their work.			
14.	Even if I disliked a coworker, I would help him or her with a difficult problem.			
15.	I help people outside my workgroup when I have the right knowledge or skill.			

16.	I am willing to do work not in my job description even if the effort means that I will have to work a couple of extra hours.			
17.	I am willing to point to things the workgroup might be doing wrong, even if others disagree with me.			
18.	I am willing to risk disapproval in order to do what is best for the company.			
19.	I challenge work procedures and rules that seem to be nonproductive.			
20.	I have tried to resolve person-to-person conflicts between workers in my department or unit.			
21.	I do what I can to raise the spirits of coworkers having problems on the job.			
22.	If I pick up some new job-related knowledge, I will share it with team members for whom the knowledge is useful.			

23.	When I think of something that will help the entire company, I will share that knowledge with my manager and/or company leadership.		
24.	I have politely voiced my concerns about something I think the company is doing wrong.		
25.	If I see a social media comment about our company that seems significant, I will forward that comment to the right person in my company.		

Scoring and Interpretation:

Count the number of statements that you indicated are mostly true.

18–25 points You have strong tendencies toward displaying positive organizational citizenship behavior. Your initiative and other proactive behavior will probably be an asset in your career.

7–17 points You have about average tendencies with respect to engaging in positive organizational citizenship behavior. It would be helpful for you in your career to seek out ways to help coworkers and the company besides performing well in your own job.

0–7 points You take very little initiative to work outside the limits of your job description. You run the risk of being perceived by the company as not caring about the welfare of coworkers. Such a negative perception could be a negative in terms of you being regarded as eligible for promotion.

Source: Several of the statements in this quiz are based on Scott B. MacKenzie, Philip M. Podaskoff, and Nathan P. Podaskoff, "Challenge-Oriented Organizational Citizenship Behaviors and Organizational Effectiveness: Do Challenge-Oriented Behaviors Really Have an Impact on the Organization's Bottom Line?" Personnel Psychology, No. 3, 2011, p. 574;

Theresa M. Glomb, Devasheesh P. Bhave, Andrew G. Miner, and Melanie Wall, "Doing Good, Feeling Good: Examining the Role of Organizational Citizenship Behaviors in Changing Mood," Personnel Psychology, 2011, No. 1, p. 204.

People who have strong prosocial motivation find it natural to be good organizational citizens. Prosocial motivation is simply the desire to help other people. Positions such as nurse, social worker, ambulance medic or human resource counselor are strong fits for workers with prosocial motivation. Yet people doing many other types of work might also have strong motivation of this type. Chloe, the information technology technician mentioned above, demonstrates prosocial motivation. The person with prosocial motivation will often have the big picture in mind of coworkers with less distress. A germane example would be pitching in to help a coworker is burdened with a spike in workload because of a sudden rush of customers.

Prosocial motivation is part of many workers' ethical code. Wharton School professor and industrial psychologist Adam Grant has conducted several experiments indicating that when the purpose of one's work is to help others, the worker performs better, or at least is better committed to one's employer.[91] By looking at the big picture outside of oneself—this time helping others—personal benefits are forthcoming.

Knowledge Sharing

Employers are placing an increasing emphasis on employees sharing knowledge to facilitate the organization being more effective. Knowledge sharing is about making some of your valuable work- related knowledge available to others. Most knowledge sharing takes place through oral communication yet using written communication to exchange useful information takes place frequently. Two examples of knowledge sharing follow:

- An air-bag designer tells another designer which features of an air bag are, in his experience, have the greatest potential for failure.
- A sales representative for educational technology products tells another rep which features of the system, based on her experiences, school boards care about the most.

Knowledge sharing has surged in importance in recent years because so many baby boomers are retiring, resulting in *tribal knowledge* leaving the company. (Tribal knowledge refers to inside knowledge about how the organization operates.) Several firms, including selected divisions of GE and the Educational Testing Service) have developed knowledge transfer programs to deal with the problem of so much useful knowledge exiting the organization.

A key part of the knowledge-transfer program is for older workers to share useful knowledge with younger workers before the former depart. Technical knowledge is often included in knowledge sharing. NASA developed a program when the U.S. space agency began to lose expertise about lunar landings as senior engineers retired. Recognizing it would need the expertise for missions to Mars, NASA asked engineers who worked on the Apollo mission to share their knowledge in meetings with new engineers.[92]

Big-picture thinkers share knowledge because they recognize that the organization becomes stronger when more people have access to the type of useful information that you would not find in databases or on the Internet. Even in a super-technology firm like Alphabet (the parent firm of Google), much of the most useful technology and product information is shared through human beings conversing with each other.

The relevance of knowledge sharing to the big picture of organizational effectiveness is reinforced by the impact of knowledge hiding. When knowledge is hidden, colleagues are less likely to generate creative ideas. Furthermore, the knowledge-hider might also experience less creativity. The reason is that creativity often depends on sharing information. A study of 240 employees, split into 24 groups, engage in metal manufacturing in Slovenia revealed a negative relationship between knowledge hiding and the hider's creativity. Knowledge hiding was measured by a quiz, whereas worker creativity was measured by supervisor ratings of the metal workers.[93] What works and doesn't work in Slovenia might apply equally well to other countries.

The accompanying self-quiz provides you an opportunity to think through your tendencies toward sharing knowledge, as well as hiding knowledge.

My Attitudes toward Sharing Knowledge

Instructions: Indicate how much you agree with the following statements: disagree strongly (DS); disagree (D); neutral (N); agree (A); and agree strongly (AS).

		DS	D	N	A	AS
1.	I have often helped coworkers resolve a difficult problem.	1	2	3	4	5
2.	In brainstorming sessions, I usually hold back from giving my best ideas because I do not want them stolen.	5	4	3	2	1
3.	I enjoy helping another person with a difficult problem.	1	2	3	4	5
4.	I would be willing to submit some of my best ideas to a company database, such as an intranet.	1	2	3	4	5
5.	I am concerned about submitting my most creative ideas on a report because these ideas could be stolen.	1	2	3	4	5
6.	I enjoy working as part of a team and sharing ideas.	1	2	3	4	5
7.	I get a little suspicious when a coworker or manager attempts to pick my brain.	1	2	3	4	5

8.	It upsets me if I do not receive full credit for my ideas.	1	2	3	4	5
9.	If I had a great idea for a new product or service, I would not tell anyone about it before I was finished with the idea.	1	2	3	4	5
10.	I have often let other people know about a good method I developed to improve work efficiency.	1	2	3	4	5

Scoring and Interpretation: Tally your score by adding the numbers you circled or checked.

40 or higher: You are generous with respect to knowledge sharing and would probably fit well in an organization that encourages knowledge sharing. Your attitudes toward sharing knowledge contribute to your ability to see the big picture.

20–39: You have average attitudes toward sharing knowledge, with a mixture of enthusiasm and skepticism about knowledge sharing.

1–19: You are quite cautious and guarded about sharing ideas. Unless you become more willing to share your ideas, you would not fit well in an organization that emphasized knowledge sharing. These same attitudes might hamper your ability to see the big picture.

Note: You are authorized to share this quiz with as many people as you would like.

Contributing More Effectively to Team Play

The Department of Health in England was recently searching for candidates to fill professional positions. A key competency demanded was the ability to see the big picture, as reflected in the following competencies: [94]

- Be alert to emerging issues and trends that might or benefit own and team's work.
- Develop an understanding of own area's strategy and how this contributes to Department priorities.
- Actively seek out and share experience to develop understanding and knowledge of own work and of team's business area.
- Seek to understand how the services, activities and strategies in the area work together to create value for the customer or end user.

As suggested by the job specifications just presented, effective team players need to see the big picture and think conceptually. A trap in team effort is that discussion can get bogged down in small details, and the team might lose sight of what it is trying to accomplish. The team player (including the team leader) who can help the group focus on its broader purpose plays a vital role. The following anecdote illustrates what it means to see the big picture.

A group of middle managers and staff professionals at a bank were sent to a one-day seminar about world-class customer service. The group was sent to the training because many complaints were posted online about poor customer service, and company leadership found this situation to be unacceptable. During the lunch break, the conversation quickly turned to the fact that the coffee was not as hot as desired, the snacks were mediocre, and the seminar leader was uninspiring. Next came a few complaints about the PowerPoint slides containing too much detail.

Bonnie, an experienced loan officer, stepped in with a comment: "I think all of you have valid complaints, but your points are minor. We are here to learn how to improve customer service. If we want our bank to survive, and we want to earn bigger salaries, we have to lean what we can do to help us reach out better to customers. Whether or not you think the presenter is charismatic, he is trying to be helpful." The group returned after lunch with a more determined effort focus on the purpose of the seminar (the big picture)—acquiring ideas to improve customer service.

Effectiveness in Negotiation

Another way in which big-picture thinkers distinguish themselves is their approach to negotiation. They focus on attaining a negotiation outcome that will bring them a long-term positive benefit, and at the same time will be fair to the other side. When people hear or see the term "negotiation", they usually think of scenarios such as the following: negotiating a selling or buying price, starting salary, accident claim, or pre-nuptial agreement. Negotiation expert Deborah M. Kolb points out that some routine situations care suitable for bargaining. For example, if you agree to take on a special assignment or request to for help when you would prefer to say no, that's an opportunity to negotiate for something of value in return. Also, if your workload expands to the point that managing family responsibilities is very difficult, that's an opportunity to negotiate for more resources or reduce the scope of your responsibilities.[95]

A key big-picture perspective in negotiation is to begin with a plausible demand or offer. In contrast, the small picture is to begin with an exaggerated demand or offer with the expectation that the other side will accept less. The problem with the unrealistic demand or offer is the negotiator is not negotiating in good faith. An extreme demand or offer will often be perceived as insulting to the other side, prompting an exit from the negotiation. Assume that you are a candidate for a new position, and the prospective employer appears ready to make you an offer. If your salary demands are 25 percent higher than the proposed staring salary, you will probably be dropped from consideration.

Yet the details of the negotiation must be kept in mind. You want to begin with a plausible demand or offer, but you do not want to lose money or another resource. For example, if you are selling a house you need to calculate carefully how much you have invested in the property during your ownership to earn a profit or at least break even.

Another key big-picture perspective is to recognize that you might want to make another deal, another day, with the same party. Consequently, you want to conduct yourself in a dignified way, and not attempt to maximize gain for yourself and minimize gain for the other side. You also do not want to insult the other side by making him or her feel like a loser. Allowing the other side to save face also helps you develop a positive reputation as having good interpersonal skills which might be part of your big picture.

Financial Acumen

Big-picture thinkers typically develop financial acumen (or "know how") because they get beyond small details to understand the purpose of their investing. Among the many purposes of investing are earning a quick profit, achieving long-range financial security, or simply having fun and excitement, similar to casino gambling. Big-picture thinkers are also are aware of key factors that could influence the future value of their investments. According to business consultant, Kevin Cope, people with financial acumen understand how the successful execution of their role helps the company earn money and be profitable.[96]

Imagine that Bruce is a plant safety engineer who dutifully executes his role. To outsiders, Bruce's main responsibility is to help prevent accidents in the plant. He would agree that accident prevention is an essential part of his role, but Bruce also looks at his job from a broad financial perspective. As Bruce explains, "Accidents can cost a fortune. Company insurance rates may increase, and the company might be sued. You also have the problem of lost productivity while the accident victim recovers. All these costs take a bite out of company profits." Understanding the financial impact of his work as a safety engineer helps make Bruce promotable in the company.

Michael Milken was considered an investing superhero in the 1980s, including being labeled the "junk bond king." He is still listened to about investing by CEOS, although he is permanently barred from the securities business based on pleading guilty to securities and tax violations. One of Milken's key financial principles is to start with the big picture. He explains how successful investors first look for major global financial shifts, and then focus to find ways to invest in that coming shift. Major movements of this type can be lucrative because only a handful of investors take the time to or have the ability to see them coming.

Milken says, "The best investors take a look at the world on a macro basis and then try to figure out, looking at the macro basis for the best ways to deploy."[97] Although Milken does not give an example of a major global shift, consider this possibility: If the world is headed toward financial uncertainty, the big picture might predict a shift toward an increase in value of tangible assets, such as gold and silver. Important details to keep in mind would be include how much it would cost to acquire and sell gold and silver, and the potential dangers of storing these assets at home. (Again, the effective big-picture thinker does not neglect essential details.)

A Few Suggestions for Action

1. Big-picture thinking is undoubtedly an asset in many facets of life. Yet to capture the advantages of big-picture thinking it is also necessary to engage in big-picture actions. In other words, you have to implement your big-picture thoughts. As obvious as this suggestion might be, many picture thinkers fall short of being big-picture doers. For example, a CEO might paint the big picture of being a "workplace where people of all races, ethnicities, and different physical status are welcome." Yet, the CEO makes not particular effort to implement a program of recruiting people for a variety of ethnic, demographic, and cultural groups.
2. An effective way to achieve a Eureka! experience, or connect the dots, is to be mindful. You quietly make observations of events around you without making a quick judgment. A person might be driving or walking though the city and notice the presence of abandoned schools and churches. The person then walks or drives through another section of town and observes large numbers of homeless people. A "Eureka! Moment" strikes, "I am going to request a meeting with the city council to see if there is any way we can house some of these homeless people in unused buildings."
3. One of the easiest ways to develop a big-picture mentality as an employee is to look for ways to be a good organizational citizen. A person can start small by looking to help one coworker in need per week, or even report broken

equipment outside his or her work area. Another approach is for the person to promote the company's products or services. One sale might be small, but it might encourage other employees to follow suit. I recall during a recent recession, a woman who worked for GM told her friends at a dinner gathering, "Don't just sit here. Tell somebody to buy a Buick."

4. Knowledge sharing is a highly effective way of being a good organizational citizen because you enhance the effectiveness of a coworker and also contribute to the good of the organization. The most effective approach to knowledge sharing is to deal with proprietary knowledge—the type not already documented in such places as the Internet. For example, a service technician might inform a sales representative, "The purchasing manager you are trying to persuade is a crazy Green Bay Packers fan. Before you even mention our HVAC systems, talk up the Packers."

Chapter 7

Becoming a Strategic Thinker

Big-picture thinking is a key part of strategic thinking, as described in Chapter 1. In order to develop strategy for an organization, you need big picture of where the organization should be headed. Big-picture thinking is also an essential part of developing a personal strategy, such as visualizing the purpose of your career. It is also true that if a person learns to think strategically, it will facilitate seeing the big picture.

One of the central challenges in of the modern organization is for leaders at all level of the firm to thinking strategically—including seeing the overall picture as they go about their work.[98] Learning to think strategically is therefore an important success factor in many positions. Leaders in sophisticated companies want managers and professionals to think strategically. A specific type of demand is for these two groups of workers to wonder about how the firm adapts to its environment and how it will cope with the future. For example, a manager working a real estate company that owned shopping malls, might think, "How are we going to adapt to the rapidly declining demand for retail space in malls? What else can we do with the space we have available to rent? What is going to happen to us if online shopping grows dramatically in the next few years?"

A strategically-minded worker at any level would think, "How does what I am doing right now support corporate strategy?" The customer-care-center worker at Samsung might say to herself, "Each time I help a customer solve a problem I can contribute to the strategy of having the highest quality products in the markets we serve."

Andy Kessler, a technology writer for The Wall Street Journal, provides a penetrating example of strategic thinking. He points out that the personal computer industry has a "radial tire problem." Kessler draws the analogy that radial tires typically last about 40,000 miles, whereas their predecessors, bias-play tires were good for about 12,000 miles. The problem for the tire industry is that people did not drive their automobiles and trucks further because the new tires were durable. As a result, the tire industry has sold many less tires in recent years.

Personal computers and tablet computers also suffer a fate similar to radial tires. Personal computers even more so than tablets, have become so durable that they suffered a 30 percent decline in sales in a recent five-year period. It may be true that many people rely entirely on handheld devices. Almost any office, however, that employs more than a handful of employees relies heavily on personal computers.

In this chapter we look at method and techniques for developing your ability to think strategically because it is intertwined with being a big-picture thinker. To begin, you are invited to take the accompanying self-quiz about your current tendencies to think strategically. You will observe that the idea of strategic thinking is similar to big-picture thinking as a result of the self-quiz that follows; similar to the test in Chapter 1.

How Strategic Is My Thinking?

Indicate your strength of agreement with each of the following statements: SD - strongly disagree; D – disagree; N – neutral, A – agree; SA – strongly agree.

	SD	D	N	A	SA
1. I often think about how world events will affect me personally.	1	2	3	4	5
2. I sometimes think about what could be done to save a well-known company that is failing.	1	2	3	4	5
3. A C-level executive should spend a part of each day just thinking about what the organization should be doing.	1	2	3	4	5
4. It's a poor use of money for an organization to invest in employee training when the company is not doing so well financially.	5	4	3	2	1
5. Before accepting a new position, I would first evaluate how it fit into my long-term career goals.	1	2	3	4	5
6. I sometimes wonder if the work I do will still be relevant five years from now.	1	2	3	4	5

7.	Taking care of day-by-day responsibilities is the best way to create a good future for an organization.	5	4	3	2	1
8.	The most successful people in most fields are visionaries.	1	2	3	4	5
9.	I am a "big-picture" thinker.	1	2	3	4	5
10.	It is mostly a waste of time and money for a group of executives to go on a retreat to contemplate the future of their company.	5	4	3	2	1
11.	Once a company hits a certain size, such as 50 million in annual sales, it does not have to worry much about competition.	5	4	3	2	1
12.	An organization cannot become great with an exciting vision.	1	2	3	4	5
13.	I sometimes think about the true purpose of my job.	1	2	3	4	5
14.	Planning for the future is an exercise in fantasy.	1	2	3	4	5
15.	If a company has a strategy department, other people in the company do not have to worry about thinking strategically.	1	2	3	4	5

Scoring and interpretation: Find your total score by summing the point values for each question.

66 – 75: You probably already think strategically, which should help you as a top- level manager as well as a strategic thinker in personal life.

45 – 65: You probably have a neutral, detached attitude toward thinking strategically.

15 – 44: Your thinking probably emphasizes the here and now and the short term. People in this category are usually not ready to provide strategic leadership to group members. They also do not worry much about the future.

How We Learn to Think Strategically

Learning to think strategically is a complicated process, similar to learning to become a big-picture thinker. Part of learning to think strategically is to develop your creativity and imagination. Developing the critical skills of a strategic thinker described later in this chapter will help a person think more strategically. Developing your intuition, also described later, is an essential part of learning to think strategically. In this section we look at a few other considerations for learning how to think strategically.

The right mental set. A starting point in learning to think strategically is to be aware of its importance and developing the mental set of looking for opportunities to think strategically. As you go about your work and personal life, ask yourself questions such as:

- What is the significance of what I am seeing here?
- What is my relevance to other people?
- Who will need what we are doing in the future?

Take the example of Charlotte, a financial planner who is also a member of the city council in her town. As she drives downtown, she notices loads of debris scattered at the side of the highway, including plastic bottles, cans, discarded furniture and mattresses, and cardboard boxes. Most drivers would dismiss the situation as litterers just being negligent and irresponsible people. In contrast, Charlotte searches for a strategic solution. She ponders, "What we have here is a civic pride problem. Maybe if we had a long-lasting program to boost civic pride, people would want to have a cleaner city." No guarantees here, but at least Charlotte can bring up her idea at the next city council meeting.

Informal learning is a major contributor to learning to think strategically. Any learning in which the learning process is not determined or designed by the organization is classified as informal learning. Such learning generally takes place outside the classroom or in online instruction, including interacting with coworkers, observing others, and picking up snippets of information from conversations with customers, and being coached. As the informal learner acquires pieces of information and insight, they become the mosaic for strategic thinking.

Ken is an executive at a chain of residences for assisted living (a.k.a. nursing homes), and he is a good listener. A few years ago as he talked to staff members, residents at the nursing home, the family members of residents, and neighbors, he learned more about the memory problems so seniors experience. The strategic insight he took away was for all the senior residences in the chain to offer assistance with memory problems. Ken thereby gave his chain a competitive edge at the time. Today, Ken's strategy is implemented by many residences for seniors.

Using Metaphors. Another approach to learning to think strategically is through by making frequent use of metaphors.[99]

A metaphor describes how something is like something else. Creating the creating the metaphor is a creative act that trigger a strategy. Here are a few possibilities:

- A business enterprise has lost considerable market share, and lost so much money, that the enterprise declared bankruptcy. The struggling executive resorts to the standard metaphor, "We are like the phoenix that rises from the ashes. We will find a way to re-invent our self by offering services instead of hardware and other products."
- A twenty-four-year-old woman who just received an M.B.A., creates the metaphor that she is like a fresh new product entering the marketplace. Her newness and originality will make her attractive to many employers. She will emphasize her freshness of her perspective in following any lead for employment.
- A founder of a bitcoin company dreams up the metaphor, "First came electricity, then came the Internet as forces that changed the world for the good. And now is the era of the bitcoin that will change how people pay for goods and services." The executive then works with an advertising firm to help promote the revolutionary aspect of the bitcoin.

Accumulated work experience. A study conducted with 703 executives points to another important way in which people learn to become strategic thinkers. The experimenters measured strategic thinking in several novel ways through assessment center exercises. (An assessment center measures capabilities in several ways, included having trained staff members observe your performance.) One method was an extensive background interview, and another was a simulated cross-functional task force team. The executives also took part in a business management simulation, and a series of meeting with various interested parties such as direct reports and a boss.

The strategic-thinking ability of was evaluated by an assessor in terms of several dimensions: ability to articulate a vision and shape strategy; demonstrate sound business judgment; and take care of global business issues. A key finding of the study was that the accumulation of work experience is related to the executives' ability to think strategically about their organizations and the business environment. Of note, having played the lead strategist role in various work activities was not more important than length of experience in learning to think strategically.[100] An interpretation of this finding is that occupying an executive role and carrying out a variety of responsibilities is an effective way to learn to think strategically and see the big picture of your organization.

Essential Attributes for Thinking Strategically

A practical approach to understanding how to become a strategic thinker is to study the attributes of people who think strategically. We use the term attributes broadly to include personal qualities, skills, and actions.

Deep Learning. To learn to think strategically it is necessary to learn deeply about subjects and events related to the strategy. You have to dive below the surface to interpret data, information, experiences, and situations.[101] Even with Big Data on your side, you still have to make sense of the facts that are distilled for your benefit. For example, Big Data might inform the marketing executive that people who chew tobacco are more likely than others to change their own motor oil, but how would this tidbit help develop a marketing strategy?

Deep learning typically involves asking questions about an event or situation or order to understand its significance. A CEO might be fed data from the HR department that too many talented people are leaving the organization to join competitors. To develop a strategy for higher retention of valued employees, the CEO and HR director need to dig deeply into the causes of the turnover.

Exit interviews might suggest a few scattered reasons such as changing positions for slightly higher pay or a one-step promotion. Yet if these same workers stayed another year, they would most likely earn a higher pay and a one-step promotion. The exit interview data needs to be sifted through to find more valid reasons for the turnover. Finally, a more valid reason or the turnover is identified: too many of the managers do not collaborate enough with their direct reports. The more modern workers want more input into decisions. The CEO and HR director are now prepared to develop a strategy for managers to become more collaborative decision maker with workers who prefer such a decision-making style.

Eleven Critical Skills for Thinking Strategically[102]

J. Glenn Ebersole of the Center for Simplified Strategic Planning Inc. has identified a set of critical skills for thinking strategically. The justification for assembling these skills is that strategic thinking is useful for making decisions at work and in personal life. These skills can also be framed as attributes for thinking strategically. The best strategic thinkers possess and regularly use the following list of skills: [103]

Critical Skill 1: Strategic thinkers have the ability to use the left (focus on logic) and right (focus on imagination and creativity) sides of their brain. This skill takes practice and is much like doing exercises, such as brainstorming by yourself, to enhance your creativity.

Critical Skill 2: Strategic thinkers have the ability to develop a clearly defined and focused business vision and personal vision. (A vision can be established for a business unit, as well as for an entire organization.) They are skilled at both thinking with a strategic purpose as well as creating a process for developing a vision. Critical thinkers use these skills to complement each other. An example is that Alison might be play a key role in developing a vision for her auditing department at work, and these use these same skills to help develop a vision for her community center.

Critical Skill 3: Strategic thinkers have the ability to clearly define their objectives and develop an action plan with each objective broken down into tasks. Each task is assigned a list of need resources (such as money and equipment), and a specific timeline.

Critical Skill 4: Strategic thinkers have the ability to design flexibility into their plans by creating some benchmarks in their thinking to review progress. Then they use those benchmarks as a guide to recognize the opportunity to revise their plan as needed. (In Alison's case, her vision for the community center might include growth in membership, year by year based on a membership drive. She might use as a benchmark, growth rates in membership for other community centers in comparable suburbs.) Strategic thinkers also have an innate ability to be proactive and anticipate change, rather than being reactive to changes as they occur.

Critical Skill 5: Strategic thinkers are unusually aware and perceptive. They will recognize internal and external clues, often subtle, to help guide future direction and realize opportunities for them and their companies or organizations. Great strategic thinkers will listen, hear, and understand what is said and will read and observe whatever they can so that they will have useful strategic information to guide them. Strategic thinkers often have those "aha moments" while on vacation, walking, sitting and relaxing or during other activities because they see or hear something that resonates and because they are so aware and perceptive.

For example, Ben might be bicycling and notice an abandoned factory overlooking a river. The light bulb goes on, and Ben thinks, "What a great location and building that would be for creating a building for loft apartments and some retail space."

Critical Skill 6: Strategic thinkers are committed lifelong learners and learn from their experiences. They use their experiences to enable them to think better on strategic issues.

Acquiring knowledge is useful for strategic thinking because strategies often stem from advanced knowledge about situations.

If Melody wants to develop a strategy for becoming a leading U.S. dealer of Chinese-made automobiles she will need loads of inside knowledge about such factors as trade regulations, the capabilities of Chinese-made autos, and negotiating with Chinese executives.

Critical Skill 7: The best strategic thinkers know how to take time out for themselves. Their time out may be in the form of a retreat. Some strategic thinkers call this type of retreat an "advance", because as they reflect during the retreat it advances their thinking. Other timeouts include a solitary walk, relaxing in a comfortable chair in the lobby of an historic hotel, or a few hours in a quiet place with a blank sheet of paper or laptop computer, and thinking deeply. Strategic thinkers also take time off, such as spending time with the family or in sports activities that do not involve consciously thinking about strategy. Some time away from heavy thinking is refreshing for most people.

Critical Skill 8: Strategic thinkers are committed to and seek advice from others. They may use an executive or personal coach, a mentor, a peer advisory group of some other group that they can confide in and offer ideas for feedback. A standard practice for developing business strategy is to seek input from a large number of stakeholders including employees, customers, and suppliers. The question might be posed to these people: "Where should our company be headed?"

Critical Skill 9: Strategic thinkers have the ability to balance their exceptional creativity with a sense of realism and honesty about what is achievable in the longer term. Melody, who wants to establish a chair of dealerships for Chinese automobiles, probably does not think that her empire will become bigger than Toyota in the United States. The ability to balance does not deter strategic thinkers for their expansive thinking. Sometimes they refer to themselves as realistic optimists.

Critical Skill 10: Strategic thinkers have the ability to be non-judgmental. As a result, they do not allow themselves to be held back or restricted in judging their own thinking or the thinking of others when ideas are initially being developed and shared. This is especially true during brainstorming to generate a flow of useful ideas. After the brainstorming is concluded, there will be time to refine and try out a few of the ideas.

Critical Skill 11: Strategic thinkers have to ability to be patient and to not rush to conclusions and judgments. Great idea and thoughts require time to develop into successes in the future to attain a vision.

The eleven critical skills described above are a lot to absorb in your journey to become an effective strategic thinker. We recommend that you pick and choose from the above list for a handful of ideas to enhance your strategic thinking. A reader might think, for example, "*Critical Skill 8* would really work for me. I'm blocked right now on finding a blockbuster strategy, so I will reach out to others in my network for possible useful input."

Make sure you are solving the right problem. Thinking strategically is beneficial mostly when you are working on the right problem. In the words of Albert Einstein, "If I were given one hour to save the planet, I would spend 59 minutes defining the problem and one minute resolving it." To be fanciful, a marketing strategist might spend months working on a miraculous new product—powered material that would become a delicious instant pie by adding water and heating in a microwave oven. Unfortunately the marketing strategist has been working on the wrong problem. People take great pride in preparing and cooking a homemade pie totally or at least partially. To these men and women an "instant pie" is undesirable because it removes a joyful activity from their lives.

Dwayne Spradin, an acknowledged expert on identifying the right problem, is the president and CEO of InnoCentive. The company is an online marketplace that connects organizations with freelance problem solvers in many different fields. A company engaged InnoCentive to find an effective lubricant for its manufacturing machinery. The following conversation helped the company tackle the right issues:

InnoCentive professional: "Why do you need this lubricant?"

Client's engineer: "The reason is that we are presently expecting our machinery to do things it was not originally designed to do. It therefore requires a particular lubricant to operate."

InnoCentive professional: "Why not simply replace the machinery?"

Client's engineer: "Because no one really makes equipment that fits our needs precisely."

The deeper question raised by this exchange is whether the company needs a lubricant, or a new way to manufacture its product. Perhaps by rethinking the manufacturing process would give the enterprise a new basis for competitive advantage. (The technique just used is a variation of asking five questions until you get to the root cause of a problem.)

A classic example of solving the right problem involved an oil spill in the ocean.

Twenty years had elapsed since the 1989 Exxon Valdez oil spill, and cleanup crews were still struggling. Twenty-six thousand gallons of oil remained at the bottom of Prince William Sound. Multiple attempts to remove the oil from the sea had failed, including high-pressure hot water and mechanical cleanup with booms and skimmers. The problem was that because the petroleum was lying on the cold Arctic seabed, it was too viscous (sticky) to pump from barges to offshore collection stations. The Oil Spill Recovery Institute, a nonprofit organization established by the U.S. Congress, was called in to work on the problem. The institute framed it as one of "materials viscosity" rather than "oil cleanup". To attract a wider range of novel, potential solutions to the problem, the institute used language not specific to the petroleum industry.

The problem was posted in 2007, with the challenge of figuring out a way of separating frozen oil from water on the oil spill recovery barges. Within three months, more than two dozen potentially useful solutions from the entire world were submitted. The winning solution came from John Davis, a chemist in the cement industry. He had experience in pouring concrete, using a tool that vibrates the construction material to keep it in liquid form so it flows easily into cracks and crevices.

He received $20,000 for his suggestion to modify commercially available construction equipment that would vibrate the frozen oil in order to keep it liquid and therefore possible to pump from the barges.

Davis, a habitual problem solver, said he thrives on the satisfaction of creating solutions to seemingly unsolvable problems He contributed to ecology by identifying the right problem Davis donated part of his prize to research about environmental cleanup, and he used another part to fly to Alaska to observe his innovation in action. [104]

Attributes for learning to think strategically. Julia Sloan teaches strategic thinking at Columbia University and also heads a consultancy specializing in strategic thinking for organizations, governments, and international agencies operating in emerging and existing markets around the world. She has distilled five attributes identified by experienced and successful strategists as critical to learning to think strategically. We include some of Sloan's findings here because if you learn to think strategically, you will develop more of the attributes of a strategic thinker.[105]

First it is helpful to have a vivid imagination. Thinking strategically usually involves dreaming up something that does not already exist, so you need a good imagination. The strategic thinker imagines what something new would be like or how something that already exists could be dramatically improved. Successful strategists enjoy intensely being imaginative when they are thinking strategically, much like a serious photographer enjoys arranging a scene to produce a memorable photo. Sloan advises us, "In order to develop innovative strategy, the role of imagination must be acknowledged, celebrated, and integrated into the strategic-thinking process." [106]

Most likely the first person to have a vision of how the lacing of children's shoes could be simplified had a sharp imagination. The shift from shoelaces to Velcro might seem ordinary today but was a breakthrough idea at the time. The application of Velcro for children's shoes fit into the vision of making the dressing of children less frustrating for them and their parents.

Second, you must keep a broad perspective. A broad perspective is almost synonymous with seeing the big picture. The person with a broad perspective both takes a birds-eye view (meaning that the bird is in flight) and takes into consideration many points of view. Talking to a vast range of people and gathering their viewpoints helps one develop a broad perspective.

Visualize a mayor who wants to lower crime rates in her city. To develop a workable strategy for dealing with the problem, she would do well to listen to a variety of viewpoints as to why the crime rate is so high. Among the many perceptions of the probable cause so the high crime rate would include, poor family structures, limited job opportunities, dysfunctional values, punitive parenting, poverty, limited police resources, and institutional racism. The mayor would then face the challenge of sorting out these diverse perspectives on the causes of the problem to develop a strategy for reducing crime.

Third, it is necessary to juggle in the form of attending to competing, incomplete, and inaccurate information at the same time. To create strategy, as well as to be a big-picture thinker, you have to tolerate ambiguity. The strategist is often bombarded with fragments of information and must assimilate the information to develop a coherent master plan for survival and growth. A case in point would be an executive, or a team of executives, attempting to develop a strategy for keeping a large retail chain profitable for the next ten years. Among the chunks of information to consider would be the fact that many retailers are closing stores recently, but some retailers are prospering. At the same time that online sales are burgeoning, they still are less than ten percent of retail sales. Furthermore, many consumers are brand loyal, while many others are not willing to pay a premium to purchase a brand. The courageous strategist absorbs the conflicting data and arrives at a strategy for moving forward that he or she thinks is the most sensible.

Fourth, you must deal with things over which you have no control. It may seem paradoxical that to be a good strategist, you need to deal with things over which you have no control. How can you deal with something over which you have no control? The answer is that you make the best of unpredictable circumstances and make appropriate adjustments. Suppose that Calvin, a health-care executive of a national hospital chain, develops the strategy of building relatively small clinics across the country to serve patients. The strategy is based on the observation that many patients prefer the intimacy of a small or moderate-size clinic to larger facilities. What Calvin cannot control is a future epidemic that creates a surge in demand for space to treat patients. Yet he can adapt to this unpredictable event by having a contingency plan for emergency extra space, such as renting medical trucks to serve the surplus of patients. (Calvin is to be applauded for taking care of then details of contingency planning to support his big- picture strategy.)

Fifth, you should have an adamant and relentless desire to win. Successful strategists want to be winners. They are excited and intellectually aroused by developing a strategy that out paces the competition. Developing strategy is hard work, and the best strategists want to be rewarded for their all their effort. Another consideration is that implementing a strategy is often quite expensive which makes choosing the right strategy all the more important. Imagine that Misty, the owner of a commercial and residential cleaning service, decides that her service is so useful that she is ready for expansion to a national level. She takes out a huge loan to help fund a national franchise operation. Misty only wins if she finds franchisees, and these people earn a decent return on their investments. Or, on a more expensive scale, imagine how much money GM invested to sell Buicks and Cadillacs in China.

The passion to win connects all of the above attributes favorable for learning to think strategically. For example, you need strong motivation to rev up your imagination or to deal with things over which you have no control.

Using Your Intuition to Think Strategically

Intuition is an integral part of big-picture thinking. In earlier chapters we explained that intuition is part of making intelligent decisions, how the intuitive problem-solving style is a characteristic of big-picture thinkers. It therefore follows that to enhance your ability to think strategically, you need to rely heavily on your intuition.

Intuition is also linked with the leadership and human dimension of strategy. Cynthia Montgomery, a strategy professor and former head of the Strategy Unit at Harvard Business School, says that many executives have lost the leadership and human dimension of strategy. She believes that strategy has become too analytical, a must- do instead of a want-to-do. To make strategy more personal, leaders should answer the questions: "Does your company matter? What is your company adding to what already exists in the market?" Answers to these types of questions rely heavily on intuition because it would be exceedingly difficult to find quantitative data to that would provide a useful answer.

To illustrate the human touch in strategy, Montgomery gives the example of Gucci. The brand had become trashed and of low value because the name appeared on 22,000 products including cigarette lighters and tennis balls. A new CEO revamped the Gucci strategy. He decided the brand should be sexy, at the leading edge of fashion, and a good value. The original Gucci market niche was high-fashion appealing to an older audience. The new CEO turned the company around to meet the new strategy, leading to survival and good profits. His strategy stemmed from his intuition about what was deteriorating the Gucci brand, and he developed an effective strategy to fight back.[107]

In Chapter 4, Detroit was mentioned in relation to the characteristics of big-picture thinkers. Detroit, Michigan provides an unusual illustration of how intuition, visions, and big-picture thinking are intertwined. In 2014, Detroit elected a new mayor Mike Duggan who was intent on rebuilding the city that had seen hard times for decades. The situation was so bad that Detroit filed for bankruptcy in 2013. Duggan's intuition was, "We can't do it by imitating the suburbs. The Millennials are coming back in astonishing numbers. Empty nesters are starting to come back. But we have to give them something unique" Two years later, Duggan asked his staff weekly: "How do we rebuild Detroit into a vibrant city with a recovery that provides opportunity everybody?"

By 2016, the city's finances were stable, with a balanced budget thanks to being relieved of $7 billion in long-term debt. The violent crime rate dropped, although did have an uptick in 2016. Unemployment dropped from about 20 percent to 10 percent. Detroit's long exodus of population relented to its slowest pace in decades and was on the path to achieving its first population growth since 1950.

Much of the upsurge, if not true renaissance, of Detroit was fueled by the intuition, vision, and big-picture thinking of educated workers in their twenties and thirties. These newcomers sense the opportunity to create their own businesses, create their own niche, and tap under-served markets because of lower barriers to entry.[108] The big picture they see is that a downtrodden city creates opportunity for growth. For example, the price of home ownership made housing among the most affordable in the country, with a median price of $37,600 in 2017. Data about the deteriorated condition of Detroit helped fuel the intuition that good opportunities were embedded in the disorder.

The intuition necessary for becoming a big-picture thinker can be honed by making a series of decisions based on intuition, and the seeking feedback about the effectiveness of these decisions. Assume that Tiffany is the CEO of a construction equipment distributor. Having sharp intuition would help her in such ways as guessing on how much inventory to have available (such as forklift trucks and lumber) and hiring the right people. Tiffany studies industry information about trends in the construction, but she recognizes that such information is only a guide. Intuition is therefore important for making winning decisions.

To begin her journey toward sharpening her intuition, Tiffany writes down and dates her most important hunch of the day: "My hunch is that the sporadic freezing and unfreezing in our region this winter is going to create a well above-average number of potholes. This condition is going to result in an uptick in demand for our equipment this spring.

More equipment is going to be needed, and a lot of equipment is going to break from overuse." By late March, the company does receive a surge in offers, and Tiffany develops more confidence in her intuition. She then moves on to record another intuitive insight and follows up again to evaluate the accuracy of her intuition.

Another effective way of sharpening your intuition is look for red flags in your work and personal life, and then later search for feedback to see if these red flags were truly danger signs.

Recall that intuition is based heavily on accumulated experiences, so looking for many red signs over time is likely to enhance our ability to spot danger signs. Danger signs are usually based on a pattern of several events or facts. The intuitive person recognizes a pattern that he or she has seen in the past. It is often difficult to spot a red flag when a person badly wants what the other side is offering, such as in dealing with a prospective buyer.

A germane example is that a very small group of people enjoy the excitement of going through the process of house hunting, even though they have no intention of closing the deal. They act with enthusiasm until it is time to place a deposit, and then they hem and haw. Early-warning signs of these house-hunting phonies include being evasive about where they work, and over-dressing for the house hunt in order to impress the listing agent. Taking the real estate agent for a joyride is an exciting pastime for these phonies. A description follows of fake house hunting that includes fraud and criminal activity, along with the red flags.[109]

A real estate agent receives an e-mail of this nature: "I am Jordan Wentworth, M.D. in Litchfield, England. I am relocating my family to Columbus, Ohio and I would like to retain your services to purchase a house. Please send me information about homes that cost $600,000 to $800,000."

A wealthy out-of-town buyer relocating to your area is the dream of every real-estate agent. An Internet search of the foreign buyer's name verifies the information. With further e-mails, he will be quite specific about his requirements. He will tell you about his family, his need for four or more bedrooms, his interest in being near a school. He might even specify his preferred neighborhood.

After five or six listings, he will tell you he is ready to make an offer on a specific house listing, the gorgeous colonial in a preferred section of town. He writes, "Please make a full price offer, unless you think a lower or higher price would be appropriate." He will also give you the name of his financial advisor in New York and ask you to suggest the name of a local attorney for handling the deal.

At this point the deal seems suspicious, too good to be true, and perhaps a scam. Yet the house-hunter wants to use a local attorney, is using a reputable financial firm in New York, and writes such specific e-mails.

The scam works in this way: The buyer signs an offer to purchase remotely from another country, and then sends earnest money to either the real-estate agent or the attorney. The earnest money will be far greater than the typical amount and might even before the entire purchase price. In some cases the buyer might make the payment in two checks, with the second for $100,000 or more. Then after the check or check has been deposited, the buyer will request that the over-payments be returned via wire or Western Union. Even if the funds appear to have been cleared or been credited to the account of the real-estate agent or the attorney, the check or checks will bounce. The money sent by wire goes to a foreign bank and is gone forever.

The veteran real-estate agent who prepared this report, advises about red flags in such a deal. In general, the usual cliché applies about a deal appearing too good to be true. More specific red flags for the real estate agent include the following:

- A foreign buyer sends you a large amount of money by accident.
- A buyer who asks you to deposit funds that arrive by check, and shortly thereafter asks you to send back an overpayment by Western Union or similar service.
- A buyer from another country, usually overseas, offers to pay full price for a listed house, sight unseen.
- The first e-mails contain many typographical errors and poor grammar.
- The buyer moves quickly, deciding within hours or even minutes, rather than days or weeks.
- The buyer works or lives on an oil rig in an ocean thousands of miles away.

The real estate agent who detects a scam based on one or more of these red flags is advised to speak to the potential buyer over the phone at least twice. He or she should avoid sending any private information, credit-card- or bank-account numbers, of anything else a scam artist would like to obtain. The agent should alert legal counsel, or the head of the real-estate agency, whenever a foreign person is ending funds, even if the funds originate in the United States. Instead of sending a refund, the agent should ask that a check for the correct amount be sent to him or her. If a refund might be sent, the agent should work with the bank to assure that any money sent to him or her is 100 percent cleared.

A Few Suggestions for Action

1. Participating in creative activities will often help you develop the flexible mental set required for thinking strategically. This is particularly true when you rely heavily on intuition to develop strategic thoughts. For example, the founder of Uber most likely did not conduct an exhaustive analysis of the satisfactions and dissatisfactions of taxi passengers. Instead he probably looked around and thought, "There must be a better way to provide taxi service than having ride-seeker standing in the street with one arm raised or telephoning a central expediter."

2. An important part of becoming a strategic thinker is to develop sharp insights into the people and situations related to the domain in which you want to be strategic. Insight, similar to intuition, stems from having a variety of experiences and paying careful attention to their significance. For example, if a CEO wanted to execute the strategy of growth through acquisition, the executive would do well to carefully study what factors contribute to failed and successful acquisitions. The executive would then have insight into whether or not or purchase a specific enterprise.

3. A difficult-to-execute but plausible approach to become a strategic thinker is to gather a few ideas from strategic thinkers you admire. Reading articles and books about successful strategic thinkers might provide you a couple of ideas. Suppose an entrepreneur who wants to develop a strategy for his or her enterprise is a fan of the late Steve Jobs

of Apple Inc. The entrepreneur reads that Jobs didn't waste time asking consumers what they wanted, such as conducting focus groups. Instead, Job envisioned what products people might be fascinated with if there were presented with these products. The entrepreneur then proceeds to develop an exotic product that people had never thought of previously, such as a video camera that records your dreams while you are sleeping. (Venture capitalists are you curious?)

Chapter 8

Big-Picture Thinking and Leadership

Gabriella had four years of experience as a customer support technician when she decided to apply for a position as a customer-care supervisor at another company. At the end of her first interview, the hiring manager asked, "Gabriella, do you have any other questions?" Gabriella responded, "Oh yes, I do. I drove twenty-five miles to come to the interview, and I will drive twenty-five miles back. How many cents per mile will I be reimbursed?"

After Gabriella left, the hiring manger wrote down on his desktop computer, "Generally good candid, but I question her ability to think like a leader. She focuses on trivial details. Doesn't see the big picture."

The hiring manager had a good point even if he needed a little more data to support his conclusion. An essential quality of effective leaders is the ability to see the big picture, not only in developing strategy but in other aspects of leadership, as well. Leaders at all levels, have to spend more time managing the big issues rather than small ones. Big-picture-thinking leaders tend to be macro-managers rather than micro-managers. The accompanying self-quiz might provide some insights into your macro-management tendencies.

My Macro-management Tendencies

Indicate your strength of agreement with each of the following statements: SD - strongly disagree; D – disagree; N – neutral, A – agree; SA – strongly agree. If you have no leadership, management, or supervisory experience, imagine how you might behave or think in relation to the statements in the quiz.

		SD	D	N	A	SA
1.	I prefer to give people reporting to me general guidelines rather than highly specific instructions.	1	2	3	4	5
2.	I send about six or more e-mails and text messages per day to my direct reports.	5	4	3	2	1
3.	A top-level manager is usually better off finding ways to cut costs than thinking about the future of the business.	5	4	3	2	1
4.	If workers have a strong vision to follow, they need relatively little guidance.	1	2	3	4	5
5.	I sometimes specify the font and font size subordinates should use when preparing reports or writing e-mails.	5	4	3	2	1
6.	If a leader focuses strongly on small issues, the big issues take care of themselves.	5	4	3	2	1
7.	I think that employees should be able to break rules from time to time so long as they are responsible people.	1	2	3	4	5
8.	It's a good idea for a leader to spend time talking with the group about the purpose of the organization or unit of the organization.	1	2	3	4	5

9. I tend to tell a subordinate what to do and how to do it.	5	4	3	2	1
10. I tend to tell an employee what to do, and then let that person figure out how to do it.	1	2	3	4	5
11. If I delegated the responsibility for organizing a department party to another worker, I would still specify the menu.	5	4	3	2	1
12. It is essential for a well-run organization to have time-recording devices to track employee attendance and punctuality.	5	4	3	2	1
13. I like the idea of timing employee bathroom breaks.	5	4	3	2	1
14. From time to time I like to stand over an employee's should while that person is working.	5	4	3	2	1
15. I have strict dress codes for any worker reporting to me.	5	4	3	2	1

Scoring and interpretation: Find your total score by summing the point values for each question.

66 – 75: You probably already act or think like a macro-manager, which should help you be a leader who consistently sees the big picture.

45 – 65: You probably are a mixture of a macro-manager and a micromanager.

15 – 44: You most likely act and think like micromanager which could mean that you would enhance your leadership effectiveness if more frequently focused on the big picture.

Seeing the Purpose of an Enterprise

The most elegant task of the big-picture seeing leader is to see and explain the purpose of the enterprise. What is this organization's raison d'être—why do we exist, and what are we trying to accomplish? A company's purpose can also be considered the driving force that enables a business enterprise to define its true brand and create the organizational culture it wants.[110] Employees want to know why the work they do is important, and other stakeholders want to know "Who needs you?" The organization's mission is slightly different because it defines what business the company is in, or what it is doing. (Yet some managers and researchers think a mission should include the organization's purpose.) An organization's purpose expresses it impact on the lives of customers, clients, students, or patients— whomever the organization is trying to serve.[111]

To develop an effective purpose statement, the big-picture-thinking leader might consider the six criteria for a purpose statement developed by Shelia Margolis:

- Is it a contribution to society—not a product or service?
- Does it answer the question, "Why is this work important?'
- Is it inspirational and motivational?
- Does it use powerful words?
- Is it brief in length so employees will remember it?
- Is it broad enough in scope to allow for future opportunities and change?[112]

In practice it might be difficult to achieve all six criteria, but at least they point you in the right direction. An informative example of an organization's purpose is provided by Greg Ellis, the former CEO and director of the REA Group, a global online real estate advertising company headquartered in Melbourne,

Australia. He said that the company's purpose was "to make the property process simple, efficient, and stress-free for people buying and selling a property." This purpose emphasizes the importance of serving customers or understanding their needs, and also encourages managers and employees to empathize with customers.[113]

Here are a couple of other company-specific purposes that might provide guidance to the leader wanting to articulate the purpose of his or her organization: The purpose of the financial services company ING is "Empowering People to stay a step ahead in life and business." The purpose of the food company Kellogg Inc, is "Nourishing families they so they can flourish and thrive."

An underlying theme to the purpose of an organization is to make a positive difference in the lives of customers. The big picture is therefore not why you want to sell your product or service to your customers, but why they would want to become a customer and how you are going to improve their lives.[114] It would therefore be possible to articulate a very brief statement of purpose that would point to how your organization could improve the life of other people. Here are a few examples:[115]

- An entertainment company states, "We make people happy."
- A medical clinic states, "We preserve and improve human life."
- A social services department states, "We reduce poverty."
- A massage parlor states, "We make people feel so good."

Chapter 8

To be highly effective, the leader who develops the organization's purpose, perhaps with the collaboration of others, must support the purpose with actions. Both employees and customers should perceive that company leadership is following through on the stated purpose of the organization. The big-picture thinking leader should ponder, "What can my team and I do to show customers, employees, and suppliers that we take our purpose seriously?"

A Gallup Panel survey found, not surprisingly, that to employees, customers, and other stakeholders the purpose of the organization articulated by the leader is less meaningful than his or her actions.

A survey also found that only approximately one-third of the U.S. workforce strongly agrees that the purpose or mission of their company makes them feel that their job is important. This finding suggests that leaders often have a lot of work to do to show that the company's purpose is real. If part of a company's purpose is to provide meaningful work to employees, it would be helpful to explain periodically to employees why their work matters. An executive might inform employees, "Here are fifty Tweets the company has received recently that show how much their arthritis pain has eased using our product."

Understanding and defining the purpose of an organization is highly useful for leaders in a business organization. Companies build, nurture, and grow vibrant brands based on purposes that are evident to consumers. For example, one of the obvious purposes of Amazon is to deliver and endless supply of goods to consumers conveniently and inexpensively. The services offered to organizations, such as cloud computer, have a similar purpose.

When company products fulfil the organization's stated or implied promises, company revenue is likely to increase. A Gallup finding is that when a brand promise is fulfilled, consumers give that brand twice as much share of their spending (47 percent), as customers who do not see this alignment (23 percent share).

In some situations what a company decides not to do can dramatically illustrate its purpose. A prime example is that leadership at CVS made the decision to discontinue the sale of tobacco products at its U.S. stores, thereby foregoing billions of dollars in revenue. At the time this decision was made, the company CEO said, "Put simply, the sale of tobacco products is inconsistent with our purpose." The CVS purpose is to help people on a path to better health.

The company's decision to put purpose ahead of profits could have been quite costly but proved to have a positive impact on CVS revenues. A Gallup Panel study found that 51 percent of consumers were neither more nor less likely to shop at CVS because of the company's decision. Of greater impact, five times as many consumers said they were more likely to shop the brand (25 percent) than not (five percent). By reinforcing its purpose, by choosing to discontinue selling cigarettes, CVS earned an opportunity to win new business.[116]

An offshoot of understanding the purpose of the organization is for the leader to recognize that careful attention must be paid to the present and the future simultaneously. The technical term organizational ambidexterity refers to the ability of an organization to take advantage of existing opportunities and innovating to take care of future markets.[117] The leader of a bicycle company might state that the purpose of her company is to provide a healthy form of personal transportation to people of all ages. Yet she must also recognize that technology might change the influence of bicycles in the future. Who knows? Maybe jet packs will finally arrive on the scene enabling individuals to fly through the air safely.

A key part of the big picture of organizational ambidexterity is for the leader to decide how much attention and resources should be paid to the present versus the future. Our leader of the bicycle company understands that the industry is booming right now so her company should invest heavily in equipment and fully staffing the organization. Yet she has to keep in mind that technology developments could threaten the present use of bicycles. The company might therefore invest some time and money into exploring the future. The jetpack idea might be fanciful, yet our leader might be concerned about virtual reality taking a chunk out of the bicycle business. If people can feel the experience or riding a bicycle down a country road by wearing a headset and sitting on a couch, bicycle manufacturers could be in trouble.

The Leader as a Systems Thinker

Another way of understanding what it means to see the big picture as a leader us to become a systems thinker. The systems thinker attempts to grasp how a change introduced in one part of the system, or organization, creates changes in the other part of the system as well. The systems thinker also attempts to forecast how a change today will affect the company in the future.

Assume that the director of marketing pushes for world-class customer satisfaction. One change initiated in the organization triggers another chain, resulting in the type of change that follows:

Upgraded product development. Tighter manufacturing standards. High caliber employees in manufacturing and customer support. Widespread employee training in customer service and satisfaction. Increased cost of product. Need to reduce manufacturing costs.

Systems thinking applies also to human resources. Suppose a leader offers low compensation to job candidates. According to the systems approach, the leader's action will influence product and service quality. The less than fully qualified candidates who are willing to accept low wages might produce low-quality goods and provide low-quality services.

Another key characteristic of a systems thinker is an understanding of how the external environment might affect the organization and the business unit. As Kevin Cope emphasizes, the environment in which your business operates is dynamic in the sense of changing frequently. A leader may not be able to control the external environment but can sometimes make adjustments to fit the environment.[118]

For example, a sudden change in tariff policy might mean that goods manufactured in another country now become costly. The systems thinking, big-picture leader must now work with the team to find a solution to deal with the problem. Among the alternatives would be to find a way to manufacture the same goods domestically at a lower cost. The leader could perhaps relocate manufacturing to a lower-wage rate part of the country, and/or automate more extensively.

The leader at the top of the organization has to study the environment in which the business operates and keep asking: "What changes are taking place that could affect our profitability and survival?' For example, a food company executive might have observed in recent years that the heavy emphasis on avoiding heavy-fat food has softened. She might therefore conclude, "Let's conduct a new campaign for our canned roast-beef hash. The fact that it has a 50 percent fat content will probably not adversely affect sales." (Another big-picture perspective here, however, is that a company does not want to emphasize food that could damage the health of some innocent consumers.)

Systems thinking by a leader can also be framed as keeping the big- picture foremost in everybody's mind and urging that as many workers as possible be keenly aware of the external environment. A systems thinker at Brooks Brothers thought about fifteen years ago, "The trend even among affluent businesspeople is away from out ultraconservative image. Our customer base is declining. If we don't want Brooks Brothers to be perceived as a museum of fashions past, we had better modify our product line. Brooks Brothers was able to modify its product image just enough to satisfy the modern conservative dresser without alienating its remaining diehard ultraconservatives. Each story has elegant clothing to satisfy the conservative and ultraconservative dresser.

Self-Sacrifice as Big-Picture Thinking

A generous approach to big-picture thinking on the leader's part is to engage in some self-sacrifice into order to benefit others. The leader thinks, "I am willing to inconvenience myself, and perhaps receive less credit, so long as my subordinates and the organization benefits." Self-sacrificial leadership stress abandonment or postponement of personal interests and privileges for the collective welfare. Self- sacrificial leaders are ethical and are concerned more about the purpose of the group than their personal glory. Satisfying the needs of the group is more important to the self-sacrificing leader than is personal need satisfaction.[119]

Self-sacrificing leaders are also described as servant leaders because their focus is on serving others. To the self-sacrificing or servant leader, the big picture is the welfare of others. A study with CEOs found, that narcissists rarely act in the role of servant leaders.[120] The reason is that true leadership usually emerges from a deep desire to help others. A servant leader is therefore a morale leader.

Here are some specific behaviors and actions of self-sacrificing leaders:

- Places service before self-interest. A servant leader is more concerned with helping others than with acquiring power, prestige, financial reward, and status. Self-sacrificing Alan is a middle manager whose group is working on an important project to improve product safety. He estimates that his group will need about three more months to complete the project. Unexpectedly, Alan receives an attractive job offer from a competitor. He rejects the offer because he believes that what he and his group are doing right now is more important than taking a new position even if it carries a fifteen percent salary increase.

- Listens first to express confidence in others. The self-sacrificing or servant leader make a deep commitment to listening in order to get to know the concerns, requirements, and problems of group members. Instead of attempting to impose his or her will on others, the self-sacrificing leader listens carefully to understand what course of action will help others accomplish their goal. After understanding others, the best course of action can be chosen. Through listening, for example, a self-sacrificing leader might learn that the group is more concerned about team spirit and harmony than striving for company-wide recognition. The leader would then concentrate more on building teamwork than searching for ways to increase the visibility of the team.

- In contrast, a narcissistic leader might be less concerned about the needs of the group for harmony and teamwork. More important to the narcissist would be for the group to attain visibility in order to him or her to receive a lot of credit.

- Shares large financial bonus with the group. An extreme self-sacrifice is for an executive leader to share some of the largesse he or she received with the group. The executive recognizes that much of his or her outstanding performance was based on group effort, therefore bonus sharing is warranted. An example of such generosity is Jeff Weiner, the CEO of LinkedIn. To help boost morale and keep talent from quitting, in 2016 Weiner gave his employees his entire fourteen-million stock bonus. Weiner asked the Compensation Committee to forgo his annual equity grant, and instead to place the shares back in the pool for LinkedIn employees. A similar example is Twitter CEO who in 2016 gave one third of his stock award—two-hundred-million—to employees. Both executives were trying to appease anxious employees, yet they were still self-sacrificing.[121]

Inspires trust by being trustworthy. Being trustworthy is a foundation behavior of the self-sacrificing or servant leader. He or she is outstandingly honest with others, gives up control, and focuses on the well-being of others. Usually such leaders do not have to work hard at being trustworthy because they are already moral. The big-picture angle to trustworthiness and leadership is that the leader the overall good is served by being trusted, particularly in the long term. Employees who trust the leader are more likely to be committed to the work unit and the company. As a result they tend to perform better and stay longer with the organization. Marillyn Hewson, the CEO of Lockheed-Martin Corp. is an example of a trustworthy leader. She has a long reputation of dealing honestly with employees, and her optimistic predictions about business results for the company are taken seriously be employees and investors.

- Lends a hand. A self-sacrificing leader looks for opportunities to play the role of Good Samaritan. As a supermarket manager, he or she might help out by bagging groceries during a rush period. Or a self-sacrificing leader might help deliver food to the home of employees after a flood or hurricane.

- Provides emotional healing. A self-sacrificing leader shows sensitivity to the personal concerns of group members, such as a worker needing to move a reluctant parent to an assisted-living facility. A recurring example of the need for emotional healing is when a natural disaster, such as a tornado or flooding strikes an employee's home. The servant leader would likely grant the employee time off with pay to manage the problem, and also direct the employee toward any company resources available for emergency help. The big picture of this type of reaching out to employees is that it pays dividends in terms of employee loyalty.
- Act as a role model for other organization members to emphasize service. As a result of the behaviors and attitudes just described, self-sacrificing leaders often ignite a cycle of service by acting as a role model for servant behavior. Many workers might think, "If our leader worries so much about the welfare of others, I can do the same thing." A study in a large retail chain found that the leader's servant behavior is mirrored through others modeling the leader and high-quality customer service.[122]

Research conducted with C-level executives suggests that self-sacrificing leadership at the top of the organization has a big payoff for the financial welfare of the firm. The study involved 126 CEOs in the United States from the software and hardware technology industries. Analysis of the data suggested that CEO servant leadership frequently resulted in a higher return on assets.¹²³ A performance measure of this type reflects the big picture of organizational success.

Seeing Employees as Owners

A very big picture held by a business leader is that employees are so important that they should have the opportunities to become part owners of the business. Enabling employees to be owners through stock purchases is both a gesture of respect for the contribution of employees, and a method of motivation. Stock ownership can be motivational because employees participate in the success of the firm as measured by its stock price. If employees work hard, the company might become more successful and the value of stock ownership increases.

A well-publicized employee stock ownership plan occurred when upstate New York Greek yogurt maker Chobani founder Hamdi Ulukaya announced a couple of years ago that he was giving about 10 percent of the company stock to employees. The company employs about 2,000, evenly split between two locations.

Employees received printed packets containing shares in the future growth of the company. The potential value of the shares was about $150,000 per employee, yet for some workers the value could be in excess of one million. What was perceived as particularly unusual about the announced stock ownership plan was that it was an outright gift in a growing company.

Thinking broadly about the stock ownership plan, Ulukaya said in a letter to his employees, "This isn't a gift. It's a mutual promise to work together with a shared purpose and responsibility. To continue to create something special and of lasting value.

"How we built the company matters to me, but how we grow it matters even more. I want you to be part of the growth. I want you to be the driving force of it. To share in our success, to be rewarded by it."[124]

The leadership team at Chobani, emphasized another aspect of their big-picture thinking, in pointing out that sharing the wealth with employees is what corporate social responsibility is all about. Employee stock ownership is a sharing of wealth between the entrepreneur and the workers who helped build his dream.[125]

Another example of a company stock-ownership plan is Golden Artist Colors, located near Chobani. The company is majority owned by its two-hundred employees. Golden is among only 4,000 companies in the United States that is majority owned by its employees. (The Chobani and Golden Artist examples are different from employee stock ownership plans, or ESOPs, which are essentially retirement plans.) CEO and founder Mark Golden presents the big picture of the company's stock ownership plan in these words:[126]

Employee ownership reinforces what employees have learned to believe all along—to act and feel like owners. We have tried to create an environment where people understand how their participation and commitment creates value for the company and for them personally. As a result, the company has flourished. We are so grateful for all the support and dedication shown by employees over the years.

The big-picture thinking of leadership at Chobani was praised by journalists and academics throughout the United States. Yet, do not neglect to factor in the little-picture detail that stocks can go down in value, and even become worthless if the company goes bankrupt.

Avoiding Excessive Micromanagement

In most ways micromanagers are the opposite of big-picture leaders. The micromanager scrutinizes most of the activities of subordinates and tends not to trust their capability and judgment. Micromanagers also tend to question employee actions and monitor closely tasks performed by subordinates. The micromanager is obviously the opposite of the macro-manager described at the outset of the chapter. By focusing so much on the details of what group members are doing the micromanager often overlooks the general picture of what the group is trying to accomplish.

Too much micromanagement must therefore be avoided if a leader wants to pay enough attention to the big picture. Yet there are situations in which the micromanager can contribute to the big picture in an important way, especially when workers are acquiring new skills. A big picture of the organization is having a highly-skilled workforce, thereby contributing to a more effective enterprise. Micromanaging people when they are learning complex, new tasks contributes to organizational effectiveness in the long run. Visualize going to an ophthalmology clinic to have laser surgery for your eyes. Would you find it reassuring to know that your laser-surgery specialist was micromanaged during his or her training for doing optical laser surgery?

The extent to which micromanagement interferes with being a big-picture leader depends somewhat on the type of micromanager.

Professor of management Jean François Manzoni cautions that not all controlling bosses behave in the same way. At end of the continuum are managers who have very high standards choose to have some degree of control. They frequently ask subordinates to rework a task, project, or report that does not measure up to their standards. The creative genius Elon Musk who founded or cofounded Tesla, SpaceX, and Solar City is this type of leader.

Musk is such a fanatic about design that he devotes hours to personally inspecting every Tesla car. He will notice a headlamp misaligned by a few millimeters. He once said that the wrong type of screw in a sun visor "feels like daggers in my eyes". At the same time, Musk is one of the major big-picture leaders in modern history. He believes that his companies, including the batteries they manufacture, are contributing to a cleaner, safer planet.

At the other end of the continuum, according to Manzoni, are pathological micromanagers who need to make it clear to themselves and others they are in the person in charge. Micromanagers of this type give subordinates little to no autonomy, and insist they be involved in every detail of a staff member's work. Furthermore, they are more concerned about details such as font size or the cost of postage, rather than the big picture. The control freak manager of this type typically gets involved in a level of detail way below his or her pay grade.[127]

An effective way of avoiding micromanagement is for the leader to learn to ignore minor actions that he or she does not like yet are not real problems. Suppose a manager prefers certain templates to be used in PowerPoint presentations. To avoid being a micromanager, he or she should not insist that team members use only the favored templates for slide presentations.

An easy approach to minimize micromanagement is to practice shared leadership, in which group members collaborate on decision making. They also have the have the opportunity to lead with various tasks and projects. Shared leadership is particularly necessary when the work within the group is interdependent, creative, and complex. A leader, for example, might say to group member Tim, "The head of manufacturing wants to install a robot in our department. I know nothing about robots. How about taking over the project of installing and implementing the robot?" The leader then must avoid the temptation of checking on most of the details of what Tim does as the head of the robot project.

One of the reasons that shared leadership enhances team effectiveness is that when leadership roles are shared, the members work toward a common goal, and may lead or coach other team members. These activities, in turn, often generate trust toward each other, leading to more cooperation and cohesion, or team spirit.[128]

Shared leadership also means sharing power (often referred to as empowerment). Meg Whitman, the former President and CEO of Hewlett Packard Enterprise, and former CEO of eBay, believes that sharing power improves organizational effectiveness. She claims, "I don't actually think of myself as powerful. To have power, you must be willing to not have any of it."[129] In practice, this means that Whitman relies on shared leadership, thereby minimizing micromanagement.

Micromanaging to the point of being dysfunctional is difficult to avoid if such behavior is part of an obsessive compulsive personality disorder (OCPD). The person with this disorder has a strong need for perfectionism, order, and neatness. Leaders with OCPD will experience a strong urge to impose their own standards on subordinates, such as insisting to always let a customer speaking on the telephone to initiate ending the conversation. The same type of leader will often be a workaholic who expects direct reports to develop the same type of work schedule.

Assuming that the micromanaging leader does not have an obsessive- compulsive personality disorder, he or she can reflect on answers to the following questions to help focus more on the big picture, and not over- control subordinates:

• How does the issue I am dealing with at the moment contribute to organizational effectiveness?

• How does what I am doing at the moment contribute to my being an inspirational leader?

• Are the instructions I am giving right now helping him (or her) acquire a new skill or insight? Or am I just being a pest?

- How would I like having my boss supervise me the way I supervise my direct reports?
- Does really need my advice or help with the task at hand?
- Have I found the right balance between being a micromanager and a macro-manager?
- Do my instructions to subordinates make occasional reference to the purpose of our company?

Answering these questions would require a high degree of objectivity. Receiving input from a trusted subordinate or coworker could prove to be useful.

Treating Employees Well as Part of the Big Picture

A standard way of talking about the big picture of leadership is to emphasize the importance people within the organization. We have all heard countless times, "People are our most important asset." Here we describe briefly two examples of how company leadership really does invest in people in order to help them and enhance organizational effectiveness simultaneously.

Sheetz may not be a brand known throughout the world, but it is a successful gas-station and convenience chain serving parts of the eastern United States. Based in Altoona, Pennsylvania, the company has a 17,000-person workforce, with more than one half being full- time hires. Leaders at Sheetz believe that having full-time workers behind the cash registers and preparing food result in better customer service, lower turnover, and more engaged workers. All of these factors contribute heavily to higher sales and profit.

Sheetz executives acknowledge that full-time workers cost more than part-time workers at first, but the former are more reliable. Twenty-seven percent of full-time hourly workers quit their jobs each year versus a turnover rate of 50 percent for part time workers according to a survey conducted by the recruitment firm Korn Ferry. The survey also found that lower employee turnover saves money on training and hiring costs. Furthermore, some respondents reported that customers spend more money when full-time workers take orders and ring up purchases. Perhaps with better service people purchase more food and beverages, but we doubt that amount of gasoline purchased is influenced by customer service at point of sale.[130] Yet friendly customer service could lead to a person returning more frequently to the same gas station.

Chief executive Joe Sheetz adds the insight that full-time workers report being more committed and are willing to put in more extra effort than their part-time counterparts. The engagement in turn leads to higher customer service, according to Sheetz human resources vice president, Stephanie Doliveira. At Sheetz, less than 25 percent of full- time employee quit each year, with part-timers quitting at the rate of 83 percent.

An unusual way of investing in workers to attain the big picture of organizational effectiveness is to lend them money deal with pressing financial concerns. One example is JNET Communications LLC, a Warren, N. J. employer of call-center workers and cable installers. Pam Dimitro, the controller observed that employees were frequently turning to payday lenders or high-interest credit card when squeezed financially.

The company began offering employees low interest loans to help pay for such urgent matters as car repairs and health expenses.

Another big-picture thinker about loans to employee is Erik Dochtermann, the chief executive of New York creative agency, MODCo Media. His perspective is "I can't have an effective employee if they are stressed and thinking about waiting tables on the side to make ends meet."[131]

A Few Suggestions for Action

1. A straightforward approach to becoming a big-picture-thinking leader is to monitor yourself with respect to agonizing over details. Instead, focus on the purpose of your area of responsibility. Delegate responsibility for many details.
2. Although focusing on the big picture is important it does not mean that an effective leader does not monitor small details from time to time. For example, an automobile executive might say to a design team, "The vehicle you have sketched is beautiful, but it closely resembles competitor cars sold at one half the price."
3. Micromanaging from time to time is an effective leadership tactic providing you have the expertise and talent in the task being micromanaged. Yet micromanaging should be lightened or dropped entirely when a subordinate does not need help with the task.
4. Systems thinking does not receive much attention in writings about leadership but being a systems thinker will usually enhance your effectiveness. A starting point is to think through what potential impact your actions will have on other parts of the organization and the outside world. For example, "If we raise entry-level salaries by 15 percent, what kind of morale problems will we be creating for our present workers in that job category?"
5. Self-sacrificing leadership in the form of being a servant leader is strongly in vogue, so is well

worth your consideration. The big picture involved is that focusing on helping others succeed is a major component of leadership effectiveness.

6. A major focus of big-picture-thinking leader is to help group members see the purpose of their work, and described in our earlier discussion of work meaningfulness. For example, the mission of the major paperclip company is to "hold the world together." Perhaps a little hokey, but everybody in the paperclip company familiar with this mission would have a stronger sense of purpose.

Chapter 9

Getting Through Setbacks and Adversity

One of the grandest applications of big-picture thinking is that it can often help you get through adversity and setback. If you can focus on the big picture of how a specific adverse circumstance is but one tile in the mosaic of your life, you will have more courage and stamina to cope with the problem. The story of a dance team director illustrates the role of big-picture thinking in dealing with adversity.

Darby Boyd had been the director of two dance teams at two schools in the Dallas-Fort Worth, Texas area. Similar to most directors, she experienced both highs and lows in her career. She was accustomed to working long hours, dealing with drill team problems, and receiving low compensation. Both schools where she taught were located in low-income areas. The students had little or no dance backgrounds, and the district gave the program limited funding.

Boyd says that in the light of adversity at both schools, she was able to build award-winning programs with over three hundred students, and dance teams with over seventy members. She writes, "I tripled my numbers in just a few years by simply focusing on the Big Picture." To Boyd, focusing on the big picture meant several things. She evaluates the program, and considers the future, past, and present. She focuses on the environment of the classroom first, and dance second. She strives to create a family-like environment. She treats her dance class students with the same love and attention as her dance-team students. Her students are the future. If the students love dance class, they tell their friends. "Happy dance kids try out for the dance team, plus they tell other students to sign up for the class." The result is large numbers in the class and the team.

Another aspect of Boyd's big picture is constant attention to the team's public image. Her teams are very disciplined, such as not talking during class. A group with that level of restraint gets noticed. Everyone wants to be part of something better, something special, and above average."[132]

We presented the story of this dance director because she represents an unusual application of a big-picture focus to overcome adversity. Go through the accompanying checklist to think about your own tendencies to use big-picture thinking to deal with adversity.

My Perspective on Adversity Checklist

The checklist that follows will help you think through the extent to which you take a big-picture versus a small-picture perspective on adversity and setbacks. In answering the questions, think of adversity and setbacks you have personally experienced. As with the previous quizzes in this book, no one is evaluating you as a job candidate for another administrative purpose, so be candid.

Statement about adversity or setback	Mostly Agree	Mostly Disagree
1. "This too shall pass."		
2. Even a minor setback frustrates me so much that my day is ruined.		
3. I deal with adversity the best I can because most things work out in the long range.		
4. To me a setback is just a speed bump along the road to a positive outcome.		
5. When I'm dealing with a serious problem, it's almost impossible for me to think of the future.		
6. Almost all major problems in life can be resolved if you are patient.		
7. If my favorite team loses its first two games or matches, I pretty much think that its season is doomed.		
8. A person who gets fired from even one job has pretty much ruined his or her career.		
9. If I am sad or unhappy, I can change my mood by thinking about how good things will be in the future.		
10. Flunking a course usually means that you will be blocked from getting a good job.		
11. One big fight in a relationship usually means that the relationship is just about over.		
12. An expression that makes sense to me when I am facing a problem is "I can see the light at the end of the tunnel."		

13. Even if I have resolved a big problem, I think so much about it for a long time that it interferes with my happiness in the present.		
14. When I am facing a difficult time, my sense of purpose helps pull me through.		
15. The problems that I have faced in life make me stronger as a person.		

Scoring and Interpretation: The higher the number of questions you answered as indicated by the following scoring key, the better able you are to hold a big-picture perspective on dealing with adversity and setback. The fewer the number of questions that you answered in agreement with the scoring key, the more likely it is that you maintain a small-picture perspective in dealing with problems. A caution is that holding a big-picture perspective about problems should not exclude you from resolving problems facing you.

Mostly Agree: Questions 1, 3, 4, 6, 9, 12, 14, and 15

Mostly Disagree: Questions 2, 5, 7, 8, 10, 11, and 13

Perspective Setting as the Big Picture

At the top of the list for dealing with adversity, setback, and stress, is to place the negative situation in proper perspective. You attempt to recognize that you will soon wake up from the present nightmare. Your vehicle may have broken down on the highway, you may have lost your handbag or wallet, or you may have broken your wrist during a fall. The long-range perspective is that these miserable inconveniences will not ruin your life.

Have you ever noticed how successful people react mature when it comes to minor setbacks and petty annoyances? They simply shrug off many of those problems that overwhelm people who have attained less success. One of the many underlying reasons is that these people are successful is they the place things in proper perspective. Some things are just not worth the emotional energy in taking them too seriously for too much time. If a potentially upsetting experience will have no real long-range-, or intermediate-term impact on your life, take care of the problem the best you can. Next, try to dismiss the problem with no further thought. Of course, it is anxiety-provoking to lose a wallet, but after you have repaired all the damage, frame the incident as a minor incident that does not damage your worth as a human being.

Perspective setting can be effective in dealing with rejection in both career and personal life. This type of big-picture perspective setting might be framed as "Don't put all your emotional eggs in one basket." A heavy form of rejection is being terminated, especially when the job is a major component of one's life. The person who loses a valued position can sometimes deal better with the situation by recognizing that the lost job is but one chapter in a career. Furthermore, many managers and corporate professionals look upon themselves as contractors who sell their services to one employer at a time, even when they are a full-time, salaried worker. Losing one position the simply means selling one's services to another employer. All of the person's emotional commitment to work is therefore not invested in one position at one employer. We recognize that this perspective is not easy to entertain unless a person has a specialty in high demand with more positions available to fill that there are qualified applicants.

Stepping back to see the big picture is a highly recommended perspective for investing in the stock market, as well as the bond market. Downturns in the stock market are inevitable, triggering many people to sell their holdings at a low price. When the price of the stock or mutual fund advances back to its price before the downturn, more adversity ensues. A winning perspective is to hold on to devalued stocks, mutual funds, and bonds because the big picture is that prices rise eventually.

Alan Skrainka, chief investment officer at Cornerstone Wealth Management, provides a few details about the important of a bullish point of view. He explains that the fact that the Dow Jones Industrial average has hit milestones of 1,000, 10,000, and 20,000 provides clear proof that the stock market's long-term direction continues to be positive, not negative. All ceilings or trading ranges are temporary if viewed with a long-term perspective. The long-term trend always reflects a rising stock market. Furthermore, the major stock market indices double about every twelve years.[133]

Looking for the Good within the Adversity

From the standpoint of emotional well-being, a healthy perspective on adversity is that it often contains some value that might not be apparent at first. The adversity might point us in another direction in life or help us develop a new skill. Many corporate executives who lose their position, yet had accumulated wealth during their executive years, take the opportunity to become business owners. Business ownership for these individuals often takes the form of purchasing an existing small business. They have the managerial and leadership skills to operate an existing business but do not have an idea for building a business from scratch.

In contrast, many executives who were terminated from their position, such as in a corporate downsizing, take the opportunity to create a new business. Many entrepreneurs were former business executives, even if they left their position voluntarily. An extraordinary example is Salesforce Chairman and CEO Marc Benioff, is widely regarded as one of the most powerful leaders in Silicon Valley. Sales Force specializes in customer relationship software and was the first company to offer software on demand, now known as the cloud. The company has close to one-half of the sales software market. Before founding Sales Force, Benioff was an executive at Oracle Corporation, the enterprise software giant. He held his first executive position at Oracle when he was twenty-six years old.[134]

A familiar application of the principle of looking for the good within adversity is extracting valuable lessons from defeats and setbacks. The defeat or setback hurts but you acquire useful insights and skills that will prevent a repeat of the adversity. Bree, a business analyst within a large telecommunications firm, interviewed for a position as a project manager within her own firm. Bree wanted this promotion strongly because being a project manager holds high status in her company and can be a steppingstone to an executive position. As with outside candidates, Bree participated in a one-on-one interview as well as a panel interview. Several days after the interview, she received a rejection by e-mail with the explanation that another candidate with more relevant experience was chosen for the position.

Bree wanted more information as to why she was rejected for the project manager position, particularly because she thought that she was highly qualified. Bree then phoned a person in her network who worked in the business unit that had the project manager opening. The network member told Bree in confidence, "The group thought you were qualified from a technical and professional standpoint, but they had one big problem with you. They thought you were too self-centered, and maybe even a lone wolf. You kept talking about your great accomplishments, but you never mentioned a teammate or your boss as helping you. Malcolm (the hiring manager) and the rest of the group were looking for a stronger team player."

The commentary stung Bree, but she listened. She soon became more gracious in thanking other people for their contribution to her accomplishments and committed herself to talk more like a team player in her next job interview.

Creating a Vision as a Path Back

Creating a vision is an application of big-picture thinking because the vision involves imagining a glorious future for the individual, organizational unit, or total organization. The person facing adversity develops an image of a better future that includes being free of the troublesome events of the present. Creating a vision as a path back to less adverse times is often used by athletic coaches. The coach takes over a losing, demoralized them. To motivate and inspire the team, as well as the fans, owners, or athletic department, the coach creates an image of a winning future.

Larry Fedora, the coach of the North Carolina Tar Heels football team is a representative exam example of how creating a vision can overcome adversity. His first full season with the Tar Heels was in 2012. The adversity in this situation was mediocrity, not atrocity, because the Tar Heels had a record of eight wins and five losses in both 2009 and 2010, and 7-6 in 2011. Yet the fans and athletic department wanted a higher winning percentage. When he was hired, coach Fedora vowed that his Tar Heels would be known for "playing smart, playing fast, and playing physical." A statement of this type can be considered a vision for a team because it points to positive future.

Fedora correctly explained that a specific blueprint is needed to carry out a broader vision. He said that having a plan is necessary in every phase of the program from academics, to nutrition, to strength and physical condition, to the custodial staff. The blueprint includes an overall plan and a mindset for everybody. Supporting the vision included making sure that great people were on both the football and support staffs understood that their overall purpose was to help the players win.

During Fedora's first five seasons as the football coach of the North Carolina team he achieved a record of forty wins and twenty-five appearances, including four post-season bowl appearances. You might regard this progress as positive, but not spectacular, and that creating a vision supported by backup plans contributed to overcoming mediocrity. Yet, this less than spectacular record provides further insight into how visioning can help deal with adversity. Fedora provides his analysis:

There are always setbacks and things you've got to overcome, probably more than I expected. But you still knew what the vision was. Maybe we had to change how we did somethings along the way. But everybody understood what we were doing and where we were going.[135]

The point about having a blueprint to support a vision can also be interpreted as having smaller goals to support the vision, which is essentially a broad and somewhat general goal. The vision to overcome adversity can point the way, but the motivational impact of the vision is often short lived if not buttressed by short-term-, and intermediate-term goals. Take the situation of a recreational vehicle manufacturer that has been downsized to about two-thirds of its former workforce, and the company has been losing money for five years. The company designs and manufactures the living space attached to a truck but does not manufacture the truck. A bankruptcy, or going out of business, appears to be on the horizon.

A new CEO is appointed from within (good for morale), and she establishes this vision: "We will become a leading player in the field of customized RVs, and provide a joyful lifestyle for our customers, permitting then to live without a fixed address."

Perhaps our CEO will inspire some employees with her vision, and trigger skepticism among others. Yet, if working with her management team with input from many workers, she establishes smaller goals, the vision might be realized. Here are some of the goals that might be set to help support the vision, including restoring the RV maker to profitability.

- Identify emerging markets for potential RV owners and design an advertising and marketing campaign to reach them.
- Make personal visits to all our dealers as well as former dealers to enhance sales.
- Redesign many of our manufacturing steps so they can be accomplished with a smaller work force.
- Find lower-cost suppliers for at least one-half our components, or work with our suppliers to find lower-cost solutions.
- Every employee will contact family members, friends, and network members to discuss any potential interest in becoming the owner of an RV.
- Reach to groups of seniors, such as those at churches, synagogues, temples, and mosques to make presentations about the RV lifestyle.
- Work with our banks and other lending agencies to refinance our existing loans at lower interest rates.

The CEO as well as other managers should discuss with supervisors and employees how attaining these short-term- and intermediate-term goals will contribute to the big picture of the company making a comeback.

Using Meditation to Help See the Big Picture

Millions of people meditate for reasons such as reducing stress, improving their concentration to enhance productivity, and to feel better physically. Meditation can also be an effective facilitator of dealing with adversity through seeing the big picture. By meditating a person can sometimes eliminate the threat that adversity brings. We emphasize sometimes because techniques of changing attitudes and behavior are rarely effective for everybody in every situation, even if applied correctly.

The big-picture link between adversity and meditation is that through meditation you become calm enough to place the adversity you are facing in perspective.[136] Assume that Chloe, a financial planner is frazzled today because she executed a trade incorrectly for a client. Following her advice, a client agreed to purchase an additional $25,000 of a mutual fund in his portfolio of investments. Chloe makes the mistake of selling $25,000 of the mutual fund. When the client sees the executed trade in an online notification, he makes an angry phone call to Chloe, and threatens to close his account. Chloe quickly reverses the sell order to a buy order for the client, but the damage is done. Chloe is stressed, and down on herself for having made a foolish error.

During the evening, Chloe invests fifteen minutes of her time to meditation. She says her favorite soothing repeatedly After her the session is over, Chloe is relaxed enough to make self-statement such as:

- "You have made only two client errors of this time for the entire year. despite the thousands of transactions you have made."
- "One error is not going to damage my career. Besides the error I made did not harm the client. The mistake actually resulted in a gain of about fifty dollars."

- "The Heck with this one mistake. I'm still one of the highest producers in the office."

When caught up in turmoil, it is easy to blame other people or circumstances. Feelings of fear, resentment, and confusion often ensure. The best solutions to these problems often stem from our own inner truth, defined as a level of intuition from where we can see the bigger picture. Perceiving this bigger picture enables us to admit what we did wrong, forgive others, and even find the silver lining in adversity.[137]

The silver lining for Chloe was that she was reminded to pause, think, and review every financial transaction made for clients. Although she was already a highly competent professional, a little slowing down in conducting business might be necessary to perform even better. Slowing down might simply mean taking another ten seconds to review each buy or sell order, not cutting back her workweek or taking longer vacations.

Researcher and psychiatrist Norman Rosenthal investigated how meditation can help people overcome adversity through seeing the big picture. Retreating to our inner selves, we can often gain the clarity necessary to understand how one setback is only a small part of our total life. One of Rosenthal's specific pieces of advice that hints at big-picture thinking is, as follows: "Try to use difficulties, setbacks, and imperfections as a stimulus to creativity whenever they arise. When you feel trapped, like a fly bumping against glass, look for a novel solution. Fly some other way."[138]

So how might a person apply this thoughtful advice? The focus is on finding a creative solution to your problem, and a key part of finding a creative solution is the broad perspective that there are probably other paths to accomplishing your goal. The following case history is illustrative.

Colin ran a Greek take-out restaurant in the downtown section of Cleveland. Layoffs at nearby companies had driven sales down below the point at which it paid to keep the store open. In the process of exploring all the possibilities of what he could do in a hurry to earn a living, Colin observed that load of old buildings in Cleveland were being rebuilt and turned into apartments and retail space. Colin then thought of starting an "interior demolition" company combining efforts with two relatives in the home-repair business. Colin's creative solution accomplished what needed to be done to regain his financial equilibrium. His self-confidence continued to surge as his interior demolition business has prospered.

The big picture for Colin was recognizing that he is a talented individual who could capitalize on an undeserved market need—aiding in the repurposing of old buildings. We recognize that it takes a lot of courage to shift fields, but many people have followed this path to overcoming adversity.

Big-Picture Thinking for a Crisis

Both individuals and organizations face crises. Individual crises include overwhelming situations such as unemployment, divorce, serious accidents, death of a loved one, a house fire that destroys everything, and personal bankruptcy. Among the potential crises facing organizations are a drastic revenue decline, pending bankruptcy, homicide in the workplace, and scandalous or criminal behavior by executives. Add to the list natural disasters, such as hurricanes, floods, or earthquakes; nuclear radiation spills; suicide bombings and other terrorist attacks; and a cruise ship being shipwrecked.

Dealing with individual and organizational crises is a broad topic. Our focus here is how big-picture thinking contributes to effectively managing a crisis. The suggestions of business writers David Sturt and Todd Nordstrom are a good starting point, particularly if you are the leader of a group. When dealing with a crisis they recommend that you should ask what your team does and why? How does the output of your group help the company accomplish its mission? Where do you fit into your industry? How do you make a difference for customers each workday?

Thinking through answers to these questions will help you feel motivated and grounded as you work to resolve the crisis. Big-picture thinking will enhance your problem solving during a crisis. Reconfigure your mindset by thinking of the big picture when crisis hits. Big-picture thinking can also help the team deal with the crisis.[139] Imagine that Stacey is the president of a business unit that manufactures and sells clothing designed for teenage girls. She is horrified to learn that the factory in Bangladesh that makes these garments has burned down. Miraculously no workers were severely burned, suffered from smoke poisoning, or perished.

Yet the crisis of not having shipments for the upcoming season is real. Stacey sits down with her team and looks at the big picture: "We are in a very difficult situation. But before giving up, let's quickly research which other contractor making similar garments could help us in a hurry. We'll also research in a hurry if any factory, anywhere has similar garments already produced and ready for sale. And from now on we will prevent a crisis by having backup suppliers for all our garments."

Seeing the big picture, as mentioned several times in this book, is part of strategic thinking strategically. During a crisis, this cognitive skill increases in importance because workers become so mired in the crisis that they see no way out. The effective crisis leader helps the group understand that conditions will soon change for the better.

A group of researchers headed by Leslie A, DeChurch used measures of historical events to identify the aspects of leadership essential in extreme contexts—those that could be framed as crises. Critical incidents, or key activities, taking place during the crisis were also studied. Published reports of events, including newspapers and books, constituted the qualitative data for the research. The extreme situations included responding to the aftermaths of natural disasters and bringing about post-war stability such as organizing reconstruction efforts.

A major finding of the historical analysis of what leaders did was that strategic thinking was effective in dealing with the crisis event. Understanding the big picture was found to be highly useful. An example of seeing the big picture would be for a leader to recognize that a couple of months after a manufacturing plant was destroyed by an explosion, another company plant could absorb its workload. Ore the destroyed plant might be rebuilt.[140]

Dealing with Being Passed Over for a Promotion

For many ambitious people being passed over for promotion hurts emotionally. Pride is at stake, and the problem is compounded by feeling upset about not receiving the anticipated increase in status and income. Yet taken from a big-picture perspective, being passed over for promotion can lead to bigger and better things. Particularly important is to be willing to strengthen your skills after not received the promotion you wanted. The first impulse is often to quit, but it is often wiser to say with the company. Heather Vough, a management professor at the University of Cincinnati, say, "A promotion turndown initially feels like the end of your career, but could propel you further if you take time to reflect."[141]

She adds that a person should use the promotion turndown to review career goals and decide whether you care deeply about filling the position in question. It is helpful to obtain candid feedback about why you were not chosen for the position, although given careful consideration. Among the many reasons for being the runner up but not the winner are interpersonal skills not being sufficiently honed, not being skilled at organizational politics and not enough experience.

A good question to ask when soliciting feedback is to ask what you could do to be considered as a stronger candidate for a similar position in the future. Your big-picture in this scenario is your future career, not agonizing about one promotion at the present. A bypassed individual might be told that he needs more financial acumen to become a division head. He might then seek to work more with finance in his present or next position. Here are a few more frequent reasons people get passed over for promotion, according to Cheryl Palmer, a career coach:

- Company management may have wanted to hire talent from the outside because they wanted a fresh perspective.
- You may not have been at the company long enough to have insider knowledge of how the company operates. Similarly you may not have yet developed a strong enough network of contacts to advocate you for the promotion that you missed.
- You might not have sufficient experience in supervising others, even as a project or committee head.
- You might not have the formal education requirements for the position.
- You might be perceived as having strong technical skills but need more development in interpersonal or soft skills.

Here are a few specific suggestions for recovering from a denied promotion, all of which have a tinge of big-picture thinking.

- Review your career goals and assess how well the promotion you missed fits them. It could be that the promotion you missed is not such a big contributor to what you want to accomplish with in your career.
- Have a dialogue with your immediate manager about how to become a stronger candidate for any future openings.
- Develop the skills you need for promotion through job experience and training. For example, if you missed out on a promotion because your spoken communications skills were perceived to be deficient, practice speaking more assertively

with people. Also take a course in spoken communication in person or online, and practice what you learn.
- Find ways to showcase your talents on the off the job. For the example just presented, look for the opportunity to head a committee or task force, and practice speaking clearly and authoritatively with committee members. Do the same thing off the job, such as for a community group.
- Learn from the person who was promoted to the position that you wanted. Instead of looking at the coworker who got the job as an enemy and rival, consider him or her as someone you can learn from. Control yourself from venting your anger toward this person. Congratulate the person on the accomplishment of being promoted. Ask the person for help with a question such as, "If you were me, what steps would you take to achieve the success that you have attained. Your insights and feedback would be helpful to me."

The last suggestion targets squarely big-picture thinking: You want to win in the long term and being perceived as a positive organization citizen who wants to improve is more important than gaining petty revenge.

Recognizing the Impact of Actions that Annoy Others
The person who annoys and irritates other people often ends up with more adversity. Being disliked by coworkers or the manager can block being promoted or receiving a positive performance evaluation.

The input of coworkers matters because many organizations based part of a person's performance evaluation on the opinion of people who work with the individual. Sometimes the evaluation is based on a multi-rater system. More frequently, an astute manager listens to what is said and not said about a given worker in spoken conversation as well as digitally. An example of what is not said about an employee would be for the manager to never hear a spontaneous positive comment about that individual.

A long list of behaviors can annoy, irritate, and create adversity for work associates, and you probably have your own list. Among the most frequent irritants are shouting on the phone, eating food at the desk that has a strong odor, regularly sitting on the edge of someone's desk, and interrupting the work of others with babble unrelated to work. Here we look at two behaviors that do not seem so serious but can create adversity for others, and backfire by creating adversity for the perpetrator. A person who takes a big- picture look at the impact of his or her actions would avoid such actions.

Being consistently late for meetings is irritating and wretched particularly when done by the manager or executive in charge of the meeting. The executive who is frequently late often dismisses the behavior by saying something to the effect, "That's me. I tend to be a little behind schedule." Sue Shellenbarger, a reporter for The Wall Street Journal, writes that these schedule wreckers get tied up, sometimes in another meeting. As a result, they leave a half-dozen colleagues idling in a conference room for ten minutes or more. (Lateness for a video conference at least allows people to wait at their workspace but is still distracting.) Not only are all meeting participants losing ten minutes of work time, but if they have another meeting scheduled after the first meeting, the second meeting, will be delayed. A domino effect occurs on the time schedule of workers who were not present at the first meeting.

Meeting participants may seethe in frustration and anger, work later, or take work home to catch up. Few people are willing to speak up, particularly when the tardy executive is the boss or wields considerable power in the organization. A study found that delayed meetings put participants in a bad mood, often hurting creativity and other aspects of job performance. Participants at the meeting that started late, usually have to stay at the meeting to make up for the late start time.[142]

The executive who is consistently late, therefore creates adversity for others, and might develop the reputation for being discourteous and insensitive, thereby creating adversity for himself or herself. People who do not organize the meeting yet are a key participant for whom others have to wait before the meeting can start have the same problem. To avoid this type of adversity for others, as well as personal adversity, the person who is habitually late for meeting, must take this big-picture viewpoint: "My self-centered behavior is frustrating and impeding the performance of others, and hurting my career. So it is time to change in a positive direction by showing up promptly for meetings."

Distracted walking is a modern problem that creates adversity for others on and off the job. Distracted driving is a far bigger problem because is the large number of people killed and injured by the drivers of cars, SUVs, small trucks, and even motorcycles. The problem is that some drivers talk on the phone, send and receive text messages, take selfies, daydream, drink hot beverages, or apply makeup. The digital hazard of distracted walking is also on the rise, often with disastrous consequences.

Coworkers or people on the street sometimes look down to text, tweet, read or play games on their smartphones or tablet computers tend to weave while walking. As a result, they often crash into others who walk in a straight line, bump into lampposts, stumble off curbs, or walk into a moving vehicle. Distracted walkers have been known to fall down a flight of stairs, walk into a glass door, fall off a peer, or walk into a swimming pool. They also will stop in the middle of a busy stairway to text, causing others to trip over them. Imagine the adversity to the driver of a vehicle who severely injures the distracted walker.

A study conducted by two researchers at Stony Brook University found that distracted walkers veer of course by as much as approximately 60 percent while texting and walking. Distracted walking is the most widely practiced by people between the ages of 18 and 34. Women age 55 and older are their victims who are the most likely to suffer serious injuries, particularly broken bones and hips, according to a study reported in Accident Analysis & Prevention. The distracted walkers often do not fare well themselves. Among more than 1,000 people who were hospitalized as a result of texting while walking, the bodily included shattered pelvises, and injuries to the back, head, and neck.[143]

Even when the distracted walkers injure only themselves, they are creating indirect adversity. More deserving people have to wait their turn in the emergency room, hospital resources are being used on unnecessary injuries, And, family members and friends have to be interrupted to care for them. Furthermore, medical insurance rates might be increased for many others to help cover the costs for the medical care needed by the distracted walkers.

The big picture for smartphone users might be that on and off the job, people need a physically safe environment. The little picture of satisfying an obsession with a personal electronic pet needs to be set aside for the broader good.

A Few Suggestions for Action

1. We are surrounded by loads of adversity in the workplace and in the outside world, such as hundreds of people losing their job at the same time, and people being massacred by terrorists and even their own government. To deal with this dreadful big picture, it can be helpful to sometimes step back from events like these that you cannot control, to focus on the small picture of what you can control. While not ignoring the big picture of problem in the outside world, it is refreshing to invest extra effort into such sphere of life as being the best parent, or partner you can be, caring for your living quarters, or advancing your skills in your favorite hobby or sport.

2. Adversity hurts, but the big picture is that almost every successful person has experienced adversity and extracted valuable lessons from dealing with the problem. Many people who went through bankruptcy were prompted by the experience to develop new habits of financial discipline, and then went on to develop such a good credit record that they could borrow money to start a new business. Did you know that Mike Lindell the founder of MyPillow business overcame the adversity of crack addiction?[144]

Chapter 10

A Master Plan for Becoming a Big-Picture Thinker

The major theme advanced in this book that big-picture thinking can enhance job performance, career success, and personal life. People who have a clearer grasp of the big picture are likely to lead a more rewarding and satisfying life. We have approached attitudes and techniques for becoming a big-picture thinker from many angles. In these final few pages we pin down twenty-five key ideas that if taken together constitute a master plan for becoming a big-picture thinker.

Master Plan Suggestion 1: Convince yourself that big-picture thinking will benefit you. Without being committed to the idea that you can personally benefit from rising above the details to see the purpose of what you are doing, you will rarely invest the mental energy necessary to become a big-picture thinker. For example, Karl might attend a weekend seminar on flipping houses. He enjoys the seminar and thinks he might try to purchase a distressed property, fix it up, and re-sell it soon at a big profit. At the same time, Karl looks for an opportunity to apply big-picture thinking to house flipping. He concludes, "House flipping might be a wonderful path to enhancing my financial security, making me more independent, and providing for my family." Karl now has extra motivation for his house-flipping adventure.

Master Plan Suggestions 2: Stop agonizing over the little picture. Staying focused on the little picture, by definition, blocks seeing the big picture. Carmen operates a profitable athletic club with 25 employees. The supervisor of physical fitness suggests that she raise the salary of all the workers by one dollar per hour, to make the salaries more competitive. Carmen does a quick calculation and concludes that a one dollar per house increase for all employees would cost $100 per week and $5,200 per year. "That's a lot of money being taken out of our thin profits." Carmen has an accurate little picture, but the big picture she is missing is that the one dollar per hour increase might reduce costly turnover.

Master Plan Suggestion 3: Analyze how your job fits into the big picture of the organization. The path to big-picture often starts right with whatever position you hold at all job levels. If you can visualize how your fits into the purpose of the organization, you have the opportunity to get started thinking strategically. Emma is a school bus driver. When asked what she does for a living, she explains that she helps children become responsible adults besides driving a bus. "You have probably heard about how kids can be monsters on the school bus," say says. "If they keep acting that way, they will never be decent adults. They may not like it when I set them straight. But I am as important as a teacher in molding the kids into responsible adults. In the words of our superintendent, we bus drivers are ambassadors for the school."

Master Plan Suggestion 4: Ask other people big-picture questions from time to time to hone your own big-picture thinking. The point of this activity is to encourage others to think of the grand implications of what they are doing which will give you a big picture perspective of your own. Imagine that a coworker says to you, "I think our office should be repainted." You ask why and he replies, "The paint has faded, and is chipped in spots." You ask if there are any other reasons for painting the wall. "He is puzzled, but replies, "I have heard that freshly painted walls pick up morale. That might even make some of us more productive."

Master Plan Suggestions 5: Sprinkle your big-picture thinking with attention to key details that could hamper your project. The CEO and founder of a high-tech company might visualize a happy workforce with loads of camaraderie that would spur them towards high productivity. As part of her big-picture thinking, she holds an open-bar after five o'clock on Fridays. The detail she forgets that given the temptation of an open bar, even technology worker can become impaired and have automobile accidents on the way home. Two such accidents happen, leaving the CEO to find another way to elevate morale than serving unlimited alcoholic beverages after work on Friday.

Master Plan Suggestion 6: Develop a career mission statement to help you gain the advantages of big-picture thinking. A specific approach to appreciating the benefits of big thinking is to begin by describing what you want to achieve in your job or the rest of your career. The statement includes the major accomplishments you hope to attain, the position to which you aspire, and the impact on others you would like to make. The career mission statement is particularly helpful in personalizing the advantages of big-picture thinking. Melissa, an interior designer might state might include this statement in her career vision statement, "I will help create comfortable, aesthetic living spaces for thousands of people."

Master Suggestion 7: Figure out the meaning of your work, or how it fits into the big picture. Similar to the previous suggestion, this activity will personalize big-picture thinking, and perhaps prompt you to engage in grand thinking in other areas of work and personal life as well. Jeff, a production supervisor of the wheel installation team at a truck manufacturer might state, "Without our team doing a superior job the wheels might fall off our trucks and our company as well."

Master Suggestion 8: Connect the dots by seeking to understand how your work fits into or interacts with other parts of the organization. Sunjay, the head of information technology at a retail chain, might spearhead an effort to introduce chip technology to checkout counters in every store. Yet she should investigate how customers fumbling around with chip readers can slow down the checkout process to the point that customers waiting to check out are frustrated. (The problem is particularly true for customers with modest digital skills.)

Master Suggestions 9: Think through carefully the potential unintended negative consequences of your plans and initiatives. A vital component of big-picture thinking is to recognize what could go wrong and take steps to prevent those problems. Kimberly, a public health specialist, might introduce a program of encouraging seniors to receive treatment for erectile dysfunction. Yes, hundreds of men swarm to the public clinic. The unintended consequence, however, is a surge in sexually-transmitted diseases in the older population. If Kimberly had thought through the possible dysfunctional consequences of the treatment program for erectile dysfunction, she would have combined it with a safe-sex program.

Master Suggestion 10: When the situation is appropriate, focus more on ideas than facts. To inspire others with your big-picture thinking, focus on your key concept, and fill in the details later. Erik is the facilities manager at the home office of a financial services firm in Minneapolis. The city experiences during the winter month, many days of alternating snow and freezing rain. He has collected some hard data that many employees are slipping are the sidewalks surrounding the building despite regular spreading of salt and similar anti-skid substances. Erik wants to propose to company management the investment in heated sidewalks. He first presents to management the concept of employee and customer safety. Management is quite interested, and Erik proceeds to explain the workings of a heated sidewalk. If Erik did the reverse, such as making a PowerPoint presentation of wiring diagrams for a heated sidewalk, he might have received less support.

Master Suggestion 11: Gain insights from many people. Becoming a big-picture thinker is not a solo act. Big-picture thinkers gather insights from many people including friends, customers, employees, coworkers, and prominent people. Add to this, loads of reading about interesting ideas, and you will facilitate your big-picture thinking. Kevin A. Plank, the CEO of Under Armour, is a big thinker about athletic uniforms, as well as about the future of Baltimore, his beloved city. From his early days in business, Plank has been a collector of ideas, beginning by speaking with athletes about how their athletic uniforms could be improved.

Master Suggestion 12: Think divergently. Big-picture thinkers minimize thinking that there is one good solution to a problem. On your way to becoming a big-picture thinker or honing the big-picture thinking skills you already possess, dig for possible alternatives to problems you are attempting to solve. Katrina might be burned out as a high-school math teacher. After years of trying, she is discouraged and disgusted with all the discipline problems, the defiance of many students about learning. Add to the list of frustrations, the school administration holds the attitude that the student and parents are always right when they receive a complaint about Katrina.

At first, she thinks of math-related occupations such studying to become an actuary, or stock researcher. She then engages in divergent thinking, and concludes, "Why am I restricting myself? So far working with math has not brought me much joy" As she expands her thinking, she realizes that tinkering with equipment is fun, and it does not involve so much interaction with people. Katrina develops the big picture that she is a multi-talented person who can be a contribution to several fields. She eventually became a commercial skilled heating, ventilation, and air conditioning (HVAC) technician, making more money than she did in the classroom. Asked if she felt a loss of status going from a match teach to a HVAC technician, Katrina replied, "Nope. I don't care about status. I'm doing some good, having some fun, making a good living. And I don't get harassed by people I am trying to help."

Master Suggestion 13: Develop your intuition. Having well-developed intuition facilitates being a big-picture thinker. Although intuition may seem like a mysterious, native talent, it generally stems from having both good common sense and considerable experience. If you make many decisions and observations in the same facet of business or personal life you are likely to enhance your intuition. Listening and learning also helps hone intuition. You see the big picture because you have been there before. Gerard "Gerry" McGovern is one of the world's leading car designers. He currently practices his art as Design Director for Land Rover, but has also contributed outstanding designs at Chrysler, Lincoln-Mercury, and Jaguar. He consistently sees the big picture of what upscale car buyers want. His broad experience in design both on and off the job, has contributed to his world-class intuition about design.

Master Suggestion 14: Develop a long-term perspective. Big-picture thinkers, almost by definition, give frequent thought to the long term. Part of seeing the big picture is to visualize future outcomes of events and activities taking place in the present. Jeff Bezos, the founder and CEO of Amazon is a heavyweight big picture thinker, having imagined Amazon as becoming the world's biggest store, and a major player in a variety of services. For many years, Amazon was regarded by some business analysts as a company that would always lose money because it continued to invest revenues in improving the enterprise. Yet, Bezos argued for patience. He mentioned frequently that Amazon was investing in developing a broad customer base and refining its customer service. Bezos was right—during its twenty first year of existence (2015) Amazon became profitable.

Master Suggestion 15: Be proactive. If you emphasize being proactive, you will often increase the probability of the big picture coming into view. Part of being proactive is seizing the opportunity see the major implications of events. Lola, the HR manager at a major national bank, learns along with other employees, that the bank will soon open a few dozen branches that are fully automated. Based on exceptional technology the branches can operate with no employees. Top management is joyous about the cost savings, as the only contact with bank representatives will be videoconference to bank associates at central headquarters. Lola intervenes proactively and advises management that the bank may lose many customers because it seems so impersonal and unfeeling (the big picture). She recommends that the bank should advise all customers that they can still interact with a bank representative by going to larger branches in their region, and the small, automated. Lola also urges the bank to emphasize that the small, fully-automated branches are for the convenience of customers who would feel comfortable with such an arrangement.

Master Suggestion 16: Seeing and attaining the big picture often means that you delay the gratification of short-term rewards. The big picture here is a major goal that you want to attain that could be blocked if you jump for an immediate reward right now. Take the case of James, a high-tech worker who aspires to becoming a project manager at his employer, a large company in its field. James has developed a solid reputation, and his immediate manager said that he is regarded by the company as promotable to project manager. Yet he has to wait his turn. Frustrated by the slow path to his goal of becoming a project manager, James conducts a job search and lands a position as a project manager in a fledgling company. He has attained immediate gratification, but his goal of becoming a project manager in a large company is put on hold for a long time. Furthermore, the new firm is so small that as promotion would be difficult to attain. James reports to the company founder.

Master Suggestion 17: Minimize getting bogged down in details that could divert you from carrying out your professional role in the organization. Details are important in carrying out any mission but a focus on minutiae can detract from attaining the purpose of one's position.

Imagine that Malinda is a business analysis for an investment firm that purchases other companies. Her key role is to provide an opinion about the value of the prospective purchase, basing her opinion on more than the financial statements provided by the company in question. Malinda also interviews key people at the company and inspects the premises. If Malinda stays focused on too many small details she observes, she may not arrive at an overall evaluation of the worth of the company. For example, in one report she noted that too many employees were eating candy bars at their desk, suggesting an unhealthy workforce. She also made note of rusted wheels on several company trucks, suggesting a company that ignores maintenance. Too much attention to such factors can detract from Malinda's answering the big-picture question, "Is this company a good investment?"

Master Suggestion 18: Be a good organizational citizen. Perhaps this suggestion sounds moralistic, but it is still valuable. A willingness to help other workers even if it might take some time away from carrying out your own responsibilities, contributes heavily to big-picture thinking. The reason is that by helping others, you are contributing to the common good, even if the contribution seems small at the time. For the organization to truly benefit, many workers would have to contribute by being good organizational citizens.

Suppose that Carlos works in the foreign currency exchange department of a large bank, and he has in-depth knowledge of what he is doing. One day Lisa a teller in the department says to Carlos, "I really do not understand how you convert one currency into another using exchange rates. Sure, I can tap a button on a computer to find out how many U.S. dollars you get for one hundred pesos, and how many pesos you get for one hundred U.S. dollars. But I don't have a clue about how the calculation is done. Could you help me?" As soon as convenient, Carlos spends fifteen minutes with Lisa showing, using pencil and paper and a calculator, to explain how currency exchanges are calculated. No, the quarterly profits for the bank did not increase because of Carlos' organizational citizenship behavior, but the bank now has one more well-informed teller. The big picture is that in the long range and organization prospers with well-informed employees.

Master Suggestion 19: A starting point in learning to think strategically is to be aware of its importance and developing the mental set of looking for opportunities to think strategically. Almost all behavior is motivated, rather than randomly produced, and therefore almost all events have some meaning. The strategic thinker attempts to extract meaning from events that other people would shrug off as insignificant. One key question to ask is "What is the significance of what I am seeing here?" Danielle, an insurance company marketing executive, is watching a television show about how sea ice is melting at a faster-than-predicted rate in both the Artic and Antarctica. The strategic, big-picture interpretation she makes of these data is that it will not be long before homeowners living in coastal cities will be receptive to purchasing flood insurance. As a result, Danielle strengthens the flood-insurance marketing program at her company.

Master Suggestion 20: Capitalize on your strategic thinking skills by working on the right problem. No sense being a big-picture thinker if you are working on the wrong problem. It takes consideration reflection, analysis, and intuition to know if you are working on the right problem. Ergonomics specialist Sam has considerable data that too many employees are suffering from computer-related disorders such as blurred vision, aching backs, and carpal tunnel syndrome. His first impulse is to suggest that the company invest several hundred thousand dollars in up-to-date, ergonomically developed chairs. Strategic-thinking Sam, however, pauses to make sure he is working on the right problem.

After conducting a few interviews and using his intuition, Sam concludes that proper seating is only part of the problem. The major problem is that many employees spend around twenty hours per week staring at smartphones, a bigger computer screen, and also keyboarding. The right problem to work on is for employees not to predispose themselves to computer-related injuries by excessive computer and smartphone use off the job. Sam and his team face a big challenge, but at least they will be working on the right problem.

Master Suggestion 21: Developing your imagination will help you become a strategic, big-picture thinker. Enhancing one's imagination is a tall order, yet many creativity specialists believe that participating in creativity exercises, such as brainstorming, storytelling, puzzles, and video games can help a person become more imaginative. Brainstorming can be carried out working alone or in groups, but the essential task is to keep digging for alternative solutions to a problem. When off-the-shelf alternatives do not exist, you will have to use your imagination. Repeating the forced-imagination process in different situations will often help the individual become more imaginative.

We return to Jeff Bezos of Amazon as an extraordinary example of big-picture imaginative thinking. He puts considerable effort into imagining what other new service could Amazon possibly offer the public, particularly if there is potential for a wide profit margin. Among the recent offerings have been a New Seasons Market offering organic meats and produce from the Seattle region producers, and All the Best Pet Care. The imagination displayed here by Bezos and his staff is not the nature of the products but the fact that they are offered to Amazon Prime customers.

Master Suggestions 22: To be a big-picture thinking leader, it helps to be a macro-manager. The idea is to spend more time managing big issues rather than small issues. Micromanagement can be useful in training subordinates and sharing expertise, but the big-picture leader has to invest considerable time in focusing on grander issues. A key part of macro-managing is for the leader to articulate the purpose of the organization, or "Who needs us, and what are we trying to accomplish?" Natasha is the CEO of a chain of dental clinics that specialize in implants, crowns, and other replacements for natural teeth. When Natasha describes the purpose of the company's dental clinics, she does not even mention teeth. Instead, she says, "The purpose of our organization is to restore the self-esteem and self-confidence of our patients and permit them to participate fully in social interaction and eating their choice of food."

Master Suggestion 23: To be a big-picture leader, you have to be a systems thinker. The terms big picture and systems thinking are almost synonymous. The systems thinker attempts to grasp how a change introduced in one part of the system, or organization, creates changes in another part of the system as well. The systems thinker also looks at the future, and how the external world will influence the organization.

Derrick is the operations manager at a bicycle company He demonstrates systems thinking when he studies demographic trends and observes that millions of baby boomers are retiring these days, and that the population is aging. Derrick then meets with the CEO and marketing director to urge them to consider expanding the line of tricycles for adults. According to Derrick, "More and more seniors are going to want and need to ride tricycles. They like the stability of these three wheelers. Many older seniors do not have the agility to maneuver a bike easily. I see the tricycle marketing expanding for seniors, particularly those over seventy-five, and not just in states with a large number of retirees."

Master Suggestion 24: As a leader, self-sacrificing behavior can enhance your big-picture thinking. The self-sacrificing, or servant, leader is willing to be inconvenienced and accept less credit and glory so long as his or her group and the entire organization benefits. A byproduct of self-sacrifice is that as the group and organization benefit, the leader will be admired for the good results that derived from the self-sacrificial behavior. Imagine that Zoey is the regional manager for a department store chain.

A hurricane hits the region, and many workers are stranded, some without food, water, electricity, gas, and sanitary facilities. Zoey works with the few management team members available to help. Instead of staying back to direct others to overcome the crisis, Zoey provides some direction, but jumps directly into the rescue mission. She even faces physical danger as she gets in a boat in the flooded streets to help distribute emergency provisions to employees at their homes. Eventually all employees are accounted for, and the path back from the crisis proceeds steadily. When asked about her heroics, Zoey says modestly, "Nothing exceptional about what I did. At our company we are committed to helping each other."

Master Suggestion 25: An effective approach to dealing with adversity is to introduce big-picture thinking by placing the adverse situation in perspective. You attempt to recognize that despite the present discomfort, inconvenience, misery, and frustration the long- term situation is less bleak. You will apply your best problem-solving skills to work your way out of the trouble at hand. As wretched at the present moment might be, you have developed an appreciation of how big-picture thinking can place you on high ground. Yet at the same time, you take care of the necessary details that must be processed in order for the big-picture perspective to work.

The master plan we have just described, along with the other information presented in this book, has been designed to help you become a big-picture thinker—a key contributor to leadership and professional effectiveness. We wish you the best of luck in this endeavor.

About the Author

Andrew J. DuBrin is Professor Emeritus of Management for the Saunders College of Business at the Rochester Institute of Technology. There he taught courses and conducted research in management, organizational behavior, leadership, and career management. He has also served as department chairman and team leader in previous years.

Dr. DuBrin received his Ph.D. in Industrial Psychology from Michigan State University. He has business experience in human resource management and consults with organizations as well as one-on-one with individuals. Specialties include career management leadership and management development.

Dr. DuBrin is an established author of textbooks, scholarly books, and trade books. He also contributes to professional journals, and online articles. He has written textbooks on management, leadership, organizational behavior, and human relations. His scholarly books include the subjects of impression management, narcissism in the workplace, the proactive personality, and crisis leadership. His trade books cover many management issues, including charisma, team play, office politics, overcoming career self-sabotage, and coaching and mentoring.

References

Chapter 1

[1] Max Chafkin, "Elon Musk Thinks Bigger," *Fast Company*, December 2015/January 2016, pp. 112-113; ChristopherMims, "Tesla's Problem: Pushing Boundaries Too Far," *The Wall Street Journal*, July 5, 2016, p. B4.

[2] "What Does the 'Big Picture' Mean?" *The wiseGEEK*, www.wisegeek.com, p. 1. Copyright 2003-2016.

[3] "What is Big-Picture Thinking in Business?" Study.com, http://study.com, 2016, p. 1.

[4] "Seeing the Big Picture," posted in *Being in Business* (www.theparadigmshifts.com), April 15, 2012, pp. 2-3.

[5] Ben Carson M.D., with Gregg Lewis, *The Big Picture: Getting Perspective on What's Really Important* (Zondervan: Grand Rapids, Michigan, 1999), pp. 44, 54.

[6] Zeynep Ton, "Why 'Good Jobs Are Good for Retailers," *Harvard Business Review*, January-February 2012, pp. 124-131.

[7] Adam Sicinski, "Becoming a Big Thinker," http://Blog.Iqmatrix.com, p. 1. Accessed May 22, 2016.

[8] David Schwartz, *The Magic of Thinking Big* (Chatsworth, CA: Wilshire Book Co., 1959).

[9] Sicinski, "Becoming a Big Thinker," p. 4.

[10] Michael Port, *The Think Big Manifesto* (New York: Wiley, 2009).

[11] Kerry Petsinger, "The Power of Thinking Big," www.yourstreamlinedlife.com, November 14, 2015, pp. 2-3.

[12] James G. Clawson, *Level Three Leadership: Getting Below the Surface*, 2nd Edition (Upper Saddle River, New Jersey: Prentice Hall, 2003, pp. 5-6.

[13] Clawson, *Level Three Leadership*, p. 16.

[14] Daniel P. Amos, "Aflac's CEO Explains How He Fell for the Duck," *Harvard Business Review*, January-February 2010, pp.131-123.

[15] Cited in David Brock, "Strategic Thinking: Getting the big Picture," http://partnersinexcellenceblog.com, August 30, 2011, pp. 1-2.

[16] "Strategic Thinking—A Task for All Employees," *Smart Talk* http://sergaygroup.com), p. 1. Accessed May 23, 2016.

[17] Based on Lisa A. Bing, "Big-Picture Mentality: How to Develop Strategic Leadership Skills," www.blackenterprise.com, July 26, 2013, p. 1.

[18] Luke Edwards, "What is Elon Musk's 700 mph Hyperloop? The Subsonic Train Explained," www.pocket-lint.com, May 10, 2016, pp.1-2; Marco della Cava, "Hyperloop May Be a Transportation Leap Too Far," *USA Today*, June 26, 2016, p.6B.

[19] Jason Daly et al, "The Disrupters," *Entrepreneur*, July 2013, p 51.

[20] Jennifer Wang, "Sounds with Style," *Entrepreneur*, July 2013, p. 52.

Chapter 2

[21] "Career Openings: 5 Signs you're Ready for a Promotion," *Jobs* (www.jobskenyaway.com), p. 2. Accessed May 25, 2016.

[22] Randall S. Hansen, "Creating a Career Vision for Your Life: Envisioning Your Ideal Career," *Quintessential Life Career* (www.livecareer.com), pp. 1-6. Retrieved May 25, 2016.

[23] Quoted in Caroline M. L. Potter, "10 Questions to Create Your Career Vision," www.monster.co, p. 1. Retrieved June 22, 2016.

[24] Most of these questions are based on Hansen, *Creating a Career Vision for Your Life*, p. 2, and Potter, "10 Questions to Create Your Career Vision," pp. 1-2.

[25] Eugene Sadler-Smith and Erella Shefy, "The Intuitive Executive: Understanding and Applying 'Gut Feel' in Decision-Making," *The Academy of Management Executive*, November 2004, pp. 76-91.

[26] Mohanibar Sawhney and Sanjay Khosia, "Managing Yourself: Where to Look for Insight," *Harvard Business Review*, November 2014, p. 128.

[27] Erik Dan and Michael G. Pratt, "Exploring Intuition and Its Role in Managerial Decision Making," *Academy of Management Review*, January 2007, pp. 33-35.

[28] Christian Knutson, "5 Ways to Get Big Picture Thinking," *The Engineering CareerCoach* (www.engineeringcareercoach.com), April 27, 2015, p. 2.

[29] Lauren Weber, "Firms Flock to Cities with Top Talent," *The Wall Street Journal*, April 13, 2016, p. B11.

[30] Tomio Geron, "The Share Economy," *Forbes*, February 11, 2013, pp. 58-76.

[31] Bob Hunt, "Airbnb Provides A Popular Use of Real Estate, But There Are Objections Too," http://realtytimes.com, September 21, 2015, p. 1; Galen Hayes, "The Scary Insurance Reality for Airbnb Hosts," www.propertycasualty360.com, January 5, 2016, pp. 1-7; Alexandria Wolfe, "Brian Chesky," *The Wall Street Journal*, May 28–29, 2016, p. C17.

[32] Clara Shih, "What Keeps Companies from Thinking Digitally?" *The Wall Street Journal*, May 31, 2016, p. R6.

[33] "The World's 50 Most Innovative Companies: 13 InVenture, For Introducing Trust to An Unsteady Economy," *Fast Company,* March 2015, p. 83.

[34] Melissa Korn, "Columbia Dean Wants Students to Connect Dots," *The Wall Street Journal,* July 7, 2011, p. B6.

[35] Melinda Newman, "Off the Streets and Into Business," *Entrepreneur,* November 2013, pp. 34-38.

[36] "Homegirl Café Catering," www.HomeboyIndustries.org, p. 1. Accessed June 18, 2016.

[37] Juliet Bennett Rylah, "Gang Used homeboy Industries as a Cover, Feds Say," http://laist.com, June 22, 2015, pp. 3-4.

[38] Rob Norton, "Unintended Consequences," *The Concise Encyclopedia of f*

[39] Shefali Luthra, "Doctors Wrestle with Mixed Messages on Opioid Prescriptions," *USA Today,* June 26, 2016, p. 8B.

[40] Justin Worland/Ridgefield, "Who's to Blame for Hot Car Deaths?" *Time,* September 2, 2014.

[41] Matt Richtel, "E-Commerce: Convenience Built on a Mountain of Cardboard," *The New York Times* (www.nytimes.com), February 16, 2016, pp. 1-5.

[42] Joann S. Lublin, "More CEO Jobs Go to Inside Candidates," *The Wall Street Journal,* March 9, 2016, pp. B1, B7.

[43] Peter Diamandis, "Abundance Is Our Future," TED lecture, adapted in "Keeping an Optimistic Outlook," *Executive Leadership,* May 12, 2012, p. 6.

Chapter 3

[44] John Humphreys, "Developing the Big Picture: Organizations Must Return to Cultivating Strategic Thinking," MIT Sloan Management Review, Number 1, 2005, p. 96.

[45] Judith Sills, "When Personalities Clash," *Psychology Today*, November/December 2006, p. 61

[46] Cited in Lauren Weber, "Bright Future in Sales? Millennials Are Hesitant," *The Wall Street Journal*, February 4, 2015, pp. B1, B7.

[47] Cited in Weber, "Bright Future in Sales", p. B7.

[48] Morgan Davis, "The Road to Becoming CEO Goes Through Sales Department," *FUND fire* (www.russellreynolds.com), December 22, 2014, pp. 1-3.

[49] Roberta Matuson, "Why You Can't Fill Sales Positions With Millennials, And What You Can Do To Change This?" *Forbes* (www.forbes.com), February 6, 2015, pp. 1-4.

[50] Croix Sather, "How to Stop Thinking Small," *http://inspiyr.com*, August 5, 2013, pp. 1-4.

[51] John Brodie, "King of Cool," Fortune, September 1, 2008, p.52; Eliza Brooke, "J. Crew CEO Mickey Drexler Would Like You to Email Him Directly," *racked* (www.racked.com), April 25, 2016, p. 1.

[52] Neil Smith, "To Build Your Business, Smash Your Silos," *Fast Company* (www.fastcompany.com), June 5, 2012, p. 3.

[53] Audra Bianca, "What Do Silos Mean in Business Culture?" *http://yourbusiness.azcentral.com*, p.1. Retrieved June 30, 2016.

[54] Bruce Holland, "The Curse of Silos, Slowness and Small-Thinking," *Virtual Group* (www.virtual.co.nz/index), p. 1. Retrieved May 22, 2016.

[55] Michael Echols, "Why CLOs Need to Bust Silos," www.clomedia.com, June 13, 2016, pp.1-4.

[56] Cited in Leon Gettler, "Breaking Down Workplace Silos," *CEO 24* (www.ceoinstitute.com), March 11, 2014, pp. 1-2.

[57] Smith, "To Build Your Business, Smash Your Silos," pp. 7-8.

[58] Several of the ideas are based on Arun Thakur, "Top 10 Signs You're a Narrow-Minded Person," http://topuaps.com, pp. 1-7; Renato Cardoso, "8 Tips to End Narrow-Minded Thinking," http://blogs.universal.org, pp. 1-2. Retrieved June 27, 2016.

Chapter 4

[59] Quoted in Matthew Dolan, "The Young Repolish Rust Belt Economy," *Detroit Free Press*, June 12, 2016, p. 1B.

[60] Denise Brouillette, "Why 'Big Picture Thinking' Could Derail Your Next Influence Pitch," *Leadership Your Way* (http://leadershipyourwaycom), December 16, 2014, pp. 1-2.

[61] Mike Adams, "A New Measure of Intelligence: Big-Picture Thinking Trumps Narrow-Minded Expertise," www.naturalnews.com, January 4, 2011, p.1.

[62] Scott Barry Kaufman, "Openness to Experience and Creative Achievement," http://blogs.scientifcamerican.com, November 25, 2013, pp. 4-5.

[63] John C. Maxwell, *How Successful People Think: Change Your Thinking, Change Your Life* (New York: Center Street, 2009).

[64] James G Clawson, *Level Three Leadership: Getting below the Surface*, second edition (Upper Saddle River, N.J. Prentice Hall, 2003), p. 19.

[65] Isabel Briggs Myers, *Introduction to Type,* Sixth Edition (Mountain View, California: CPP, Inc., 1998), p. 9.

[66] Quoted in Michelle Goodman, "Lessons Unlearned: Six Lies They Teach in Business School," *Entrepreneur*, May 2015, p. 58.

[67] Quoted in Goodman, "Lessons Unlearned," p. 58.

[68] "Getting the Big Picture and Paying Attention to the Details," http://faculty.bucks.edu, May 10, 201, p. 1.

[69] Research of Damasio reported in Karen Weintraub, "Inner Workings of a Creative Brain," *USA Today*, November 9, 2013; Amy Novotney, "No Such thing as 'Right-Brained' or 'Left-Brained,' New Research Finds," *Monitor on Psychology*, November 2013, p. 10.

[70] "Getting the Big Picture and Paying Attention to Details," p. 1.

[71] Teresa M. Amabile, "How to Kill Creativity," *Harvard Business Review*, September-October 1998, pp. 78-79

[72] "Starbucks: More than a Caffeine High," *Executive Leadership*, August 2006, p. 4.

Chapter 5

[73] Experiments summarized in Denise Cummins, "How to Boost Your Willpower," *Psychology Today* (www.psychologytoday.com/blog), June 21, 2013, p. 1.

[74] Experiment summarized in Regina Conti, "Delay of Gratification," www.briticanna.com, Updated December 21, 2015, p. 2.

[75] Ben Carson, M.D., with Greg Lewis, *The Big Picture: Getting Perspective on What's Really Important* (New York: Zondervan, 1999), pp. 123, 125, 132.

[76] Christopher Atwell, "See it. Plan it, Do it: How a Young Marketing Professional Strategized her Way to CMO," *Black Enterprise*, February 2014, p. 41.

[77] Russ Harris, *The Confidence Gap: A Guide to Overcoming Fear and Self-Doubt* (Boston, MA: 2011).

[78] Bill Gordon, "Delayed Gratification: A Battle That Must Be Won," www.psychologytoday.com), January 11, 2014, p. 6.

[79] Stephen Kotler, "Escape Artists," *Psychology Today*, September/October 2009, pp. 73-75.

[80] Research summarized in Conti, "Delay of Gratification," p. 3;David C. Blunder and Jack Block, "The Role of Ego-Control Ego-Resiliency, and I Q in Delay of Gratification in Adolescence," *Journal of Personality and Social Psychology,* December1989, pp. 1041-1056.

[81] Joe Robinson, "Where there's Willpower, there's a Way," *Entrepreneur*, July 2015, p. 52.

[82] Angela Duckworth, Christopher Peterson, Michael D. Matthews, and Dennis B. Kelly, "Grit: Perseverance and Passion for Long-Term Goals," *Journal of Personality and Social Psychology*, No. 6, 2007, pp. 1087-1101; Duckworth, "Grit: Perseverance and Passion for Long-Term Goals," www.sdgva.org, December 4, 2013, pp. 1=3; Angela Duckworth and Lauren Eskreis-Winkler, "True Grit," *Observer* (www.psychologicalscience.org), Vol. 26, No. 4, April 2013, pp. 1-3.

[83] Robert Harrow, "Average Credit Card Debt in America: 2016 Facts and Figures," www.valuepenguin.com, November 28, 2016, pp. 2-3.

[84] Cited in Lydia Dallett, "Mastering Delayed Gratification Is the Key to Financial Success," *Business Insider* (www.businessinsider.com), January 24, 2014, pp. 1-2.

[85] The suggestions include some of the ideas contained in Brendan Baker, "5 Strategies for Delayed Gratification and Why You should Do It," www.startofhappiness.co, November 19, 2012, pp. 6-7; "Delaying Gratification—5 Tips On How to Delay Gratification," *Financial Highway* (www.financialhighway.com), pp. 2-4.

Chapter 6

[86] Karen Burns, "How Seeing the 'Big Picture' Can Help Your Career," *U.S, News* (http://money.usnews.com), January 21, 2009, p. 1.

[87] Joe Robinson, "The Rule-Breakers," *Entrepreneur,* October 2015, pp. 50-52.

[88] Bruce Grierson, "Eureka! *Psychology Today,* March/April 2015, pp. 48-57.

[89] Todd Clausen, "Fleet Feet Will Set the Pace with $20 Minimum Wage," *Democrat and Chronicle,* January 15, 2017, pp. 1E, 4E.

[90] "Design Is Changing How We Innovate," (Denis Dekovic) *Fast Company,* October, 2014, p. 52.

[91] Joel Koopman, Klodiana Lanaj, and Brent A. Scott, "Integrating the Bright and Dark Sides of OCB: A Daily Investigation of the Benefits and Costs of Helping Others," *Academy of Management Journal,* April 2016, pp. 414-435; Scott B. MacKenzie, Philip M. Podaskoff, and Nathan P. Podaskoff, "Challenge-Oriented Organizational Citizenship Behaviors and Organizational Effectiveness: Do Challenge-Oriented Behaviors Really Have an Impact on the Organization's Bottom Line?" *Personnel Psychology,* No. 3, 2011, pp. 559–592.

[92] Research cited in Susan Dominus, "Is Giving the Secret to Getting Ahead," *The New York Times* (www.nytimes.com), March 27, 2013; Adam M. Grant and John J. Sumanth, "Mission Possible? The Performance of Pro-socially Motivated Employees Depends on Manager Trustworthiness," *Journal of Applied Psychology,* July 2009, pp. 927-944.

[93] "Chowing Down on Boomers' Brains," *Bloomberg Businessweek,* January 25-31, 2016 pp. 19-20.

[94] Matej Cerne, et al, "What Goes Around Comes Around: Knowledge Hiding, Perceived Motivational Climate, and Creativity," *Academy of Management Journal,* February 2014, pp. 172-192.

[95] "What We are Looking for: Department of Health—Higher Executive

Officer," *Department of Health* (www.5.i-grasp.com), 2016.

[96] Deborah M. Kolb, "Managing Yourself: Be Your Own Best Advocate," *Harvard Business Review*, November 2015, pp.130-133.

[97] Kevin Cope, *Seeing the Big Picture: Business Acumen to Build Your Credibility, Career, and Company* (Austin, TX: Greenleaf Book Group LLC, 2012).

[98] Matt Krantz, "5 Tips from a 1980s Investing Superhero," *USA Today Money*, May 29, 2016, p. 6B.

Chapter 7

[99] James R. Bailey, "The Mind of the Strategist," *Academy of Management Learning and Education,* December 2003, p. 385.

[100] Andy Kessler, "The Radial Tire Lesson for Tech," *The Wall Street Journal*, June 3, 2017, p. A17.

[101] Julia Sloan, *Learning to Think Strategically* (London and New York: Routledge, 2014), pp. 55-56.

[102] Lisa Dragoni, In-Sue Oh, Paul Vankatwyk, and Paul E. Tesluk, "Developing Executive Leaders: The Relative Contribution of Cognitive Ability, Personality, and the Accumulation of Work Experience in Predicting Strategic Thinking Competency," *Personnel Psychology*, Number 4, 2011, pp. 829-864.

[103] Sloan, *Learning to think Strategically,* p. 97.

[104] Adapted with permission from J. Glenn Ebersole, "Strategic thinking: 11 Critical Skills Needed," *Course and Direction* (www.casp.com ©Copyright 2016 by Center for Strategic Planning Inc., pp. 1-2. The examples in this section, however, are original.

[105] Dwayne Spradlin, "Are You Solving the Right Problem?" *Harvard Business Review*, September 2012, pp. 85-87.

[106] Julia Sloan, *Learning to Think Strategically* (London and New York Routledge, 2014), pp. 215-229.

[107] Sloan, *Learning to Think Strategically*, p. 221.

[108] "A Conversation with Cynthia Montgomery: How We Think about Strategy," *Executive Leadership*, June 12, p. 3; Cynthia Montgomery, "Putting Leadership Back in Strategy," *Harvard Business Review*, January 2 008, pp. 54-80.

[109] Adapted from Pzarov, "Real Estate Scam Warning!" *Homestead's Blog* (https: //homesteadtitle.wordpress.com), June 15, 2010, pp. 1-2.

Chapter 8

[110] Nate Dvorak and Bryant Ott, "A Company's Purpose Has to Be a Lot More than Words," www.gallup.com, July 28, 2015, pp.1-5.

[111] Elsbeth Johnson, How Leaders Can Focus on the Big Picture," *Harvard Business Review* (https://hbr.org), November 9, 2016, p. 1.

[112] The first three are adapted from Shelia Margolis, "Purpose of an Organization," © 2017 (https://sheliamargolis.com), p.2. ©2017 Shelia Margolis., p. 3.

[113] Graham Kenny, "Your Company's Purpose Is Not Its Vision, Mission, or Values," *Harvard Business Review* (https://hbr.org), September 3, 2014, p. 3.

[114] Michelle Shemilt, "Are You Really Seeing the Big Picture?" www.entrepreneur.com, January 22, 2014, pp. 3-4.

[115] The first three are adapted from Margolis, "Purpose of an Organization," p. 3.

[116] The references to Gallup in this section are from Dvorak and Ott, "A Company's Purpose Has to Be a Lot More than Words," July 28, 2015, pp. 1-

4.

[117] Julian Birkinshaw and Kamini Guptak, "Clarifying the Distinctive Contribution of Ambidexterity to the Field of Organization Studies," *Academy of Management Perspective*, November 2013, pp. 287-298

[118] Kevin Cope, *Seeing the Big Picture: Business Acumen to Build Your Credibility, Career, and Company* (Austin, TX: Greenleaf Book Group Press, 2012), pp, 102, 104.

[119] David De Cremer et al, "When Does Self-Sacrificial Leadership Motivate Prosocial Behavior? It Depends on Followers' Prevention Focus," *Journal of Applied Psychology*, July 2009, pp. 887-899.

[120] Suzanne J. Peterson, Benjamin M. Galvin, and Donald Lange, "CEO Servant Leadership: Exploring Executive Characteristics and Firm Performance," *Personnel Psychology*, No. 3, 2012, p. 585.

[121] Kerry Close, "LinkedIn's CEO is Giving His entire $14 Million bonus to His Employees," *Money* (http://time.com/money, March 3, 2016, pp. 1-3.

[122] Emily Hunter et al, "Servant Leaders Inspire Servant Followers: Antecedents for Employees and the Organization," *The Leadership Quarterly*, April 2013, pp. 316-331.

[123] Peterson, Galvin, and Lange, "CEO Servant Leadership," pp.580.

[124] Paul Davidson, "Chobani Workers Get Ownership Stake that Could Make them Millionaires," *USA Today* (www.usatoday.com), April 27, 2016, p. 1.

[125] Joseph R. Biasi, "What Chobani Employee Stock Ownership Plan Means for the Middle Class?" *www.thehuffingtonpost.com*, May 1, 2016, p. 2.

[126] David Hill, "Chobani Entering World of Employee Ownership," *Binghamton Press & Sun Bulletin*, May 23, 2016. p. 7A.

[127] Amy Gallo, "Stop Being Micromanaged," *Harvard Business Review* (https://hbr.org), September 25, 2011, pp. 2-3 Manzoni is cited in this source, but the examples presented are original.

[128] Danni Wang, David A. Waldman, and Zhen Zhang, "A Meta-Analysis of Shared Leadership and Team Effectiveness," *Journal of Applied Psychology*, March 2014, p. 191.

[129] Patricia Sellers, "eBay's Secret," *Fortune*, October 18, 2004, p. 161.

[130] Rachel Feintzeig, "Full-time Hires Buck Trend at Some Firms," *The Wall Street Journal*, April 27, 2016, pp. B1, B7.

[131] Rachel Emma Silverman, "Bosses Turn to Loans to Help Employees," *The Wall Street Journal*, June 1, 2016, p. B5.

[132] Darby Boyd, "Seeing the 'Big Picture'," www.madance.com, pp. 1-3. Retrieved February 4, 2017; "Making the Cut—Katy's ISD's Dance and Drill Teams," www.katymagazine.com, September 3, 2015, pp. 1-3.

[133] Quoted in Adam Shell, "Major Dow Benchmark," *USA Today*, February 6, 2017, p. 4B.

[134] Alex Konrad, "Nonstop Benioff," *Forbes*, September 13, 2016, pp. 84, 88-98.

[135] Adrian Hale, "Blazing a Path of Hope," *Democrat and Chronicle,* February 5, 2017, p. 29A.

[136] Ross Martin, "Big Picture: Fedora Discusses his Plan, Adversity," *Carolina Blue News* (http://northcrolina247/sports. com), December 3, 2015, pp. 1-2.

[137] Ross Martin, "Big Picture: Fedora Discusses His Plan, Adversity," *Carolina Blue News* (http://northcrolina247/sports. com), December 3, 2015, pp. 1-2.

[138] Quoted in Jeanne Ball, "3 Ways Transcendental Meditation Helps Your

Deal with Adversity," www.tm.org/blog/meditation, December 15, 2015, pp. 1-5.

[139] David Sturt and Todd Nordstrom, "Grab a Spoon—Lessons from Nutella about Adversity and Success," Forbes (www.Forbes.com), July 6, 2016, p. 6.

[140] Leslie A. DeChurch et al, "A Historiometric Analysis of Leadership in Mission Critical Multiteam Environments," The Leadership Quarterly, February 2011, pp. 152-169.

[141] Quoted in Joann S. Lublin, Passed over for a Promotion? Here are Next Steps," The Wall Street Journal, April 20, 2016, p.D2. Several of the other ideas in this section are based on and adapted from the Lublin article, as well as from Debra Auerbach, "Learning from Not Getting Promoted," CareerBuilder, published in Democrat and Chronicle, October 20, 2013, p. 2F.

[142] Sue Shellenbarger, "Don't Be Late or You'll Be a Schedule Wrecker," The Wall Street Journal, July 8, 2015, pp. D1, D3.

[143] Several of the facts and observations in this section are from Jane E. Brody, "Distracted Walkers Pose Threat to Self and Others," The New York Times (http://well.blogs.nytimes.com), December 7, 2015, pp. 1-4.

[144] Josh Dean, "The Preposterous Entrepreneurial Success Story of Mike Lindell," BloombergBusinessweek, January 10–January 22, 2017, pp. 52-57.

www.ingramcontent.com/pod-product-compliance
Lightning Source LLC
LaVergne TN
LVHW041611070426
835507LV00008B/186